MW00423375

The Three B's

How to Build An Event Planning Business

Build Your Business

Build Your Bank Account

Build Your Legacy

by Valerie Jenkins

FIRST EDITION: April 2021

Paperback ISBN 978-1-7370336-0-8

Ebook ISBN 978-1-7370336-1-5

To the souls that spoke life into my gifts, my mind,
and my spirit; thank you.

Sarah Jenkins, Robert L. Jenkins Sr.,
and Evelyn Jenkins

TABLE OF CONTENTS

SECTION 1

Purpose

INTRODUCTION

The Purpose Behind An Event

E verything is combined. When we look at the existence of anything, we can see that it has a purpose, an order, and a function. There is nothing that lives inside of nature that doesn't work alongside all of creation. The sun's mission is to measure the time of day while the moon functions as our clock at night. The greater light, i.e., the sun also provides warmth and vitamins to every living creature on earth.

Meanwhile, the waters help create the cycle for our clouds to exist and feed the plants that need rain. Our world, our lives, exist inside of cycles. We are no different as humans. Each of us contains a gifting, a skillset, a predetermined mission, and a personality set. It's in the combination of these things where our purpose lives and thrives.

Most importantly, it's inside our purpose that we see how to be co-creators with one another. There is no person alive or dead that existed without such a thing. If we operated for ourselves and within ourselves, we'd each possess the ability to do everything.

We'd all be organizational, keen at cooking, amazing mechanics, singers, technologically savvy, green-thumbed, dancers that can write books, speak every language, decode every mathematical challenge, and have superhuman strength. We'd all be quick learners because we'd be teachers of every subject. We would not need to mate, love, protect, or encompass another human being. Our very lives would begin and stop with "I." Hallelujah, that isn't the case.

It took me quite a while to step into this realization. For years, I ran away from my light because of the voices of others, the outside world, etc. So I fought my purpose every time it tried to creep its way out of me. The moment I felt that pull towards greater, I'd take my backhand and smack it back down into submission. That light would turn on, and I'd crumble because of past shame, guilt, and feeling as though my voice and calling wasn't worth ten dimes. I wasn't ready to acknowledge its existence, nor was I prepared to accept it was meant for me. In hindsight, I see how disrespectful my running was. My heavenly father was presenting me with a gift, and all I had to do was be brave enough to open it and accept what was inside.

Had I opened my special gift earlier, I would've learned that operating in your purpose is a lifetime commitment to evolving. I would have seen that I was receiving a new box ever so often, and I'd never stop getting them until I was taken up to Heaven. That's a lesson so many of us forget or never learn. Stepping into our purpose is a continual development process. It requires an everyday mindset that says, "I'm going to be purposeful every day. I'm going to serve others every day." I'm going to think like this should never allow you to wake up and say, "This is just who I am." Operating in your calling will take you through stages of unlearning, relearning, and establishing new thought patterns and beliefs. There are levels to this. Even I'm still growing in it.

Knowing what I was put on this earth to do was my turning point. It opened my eyes to see that purpose is always about other people. There isn't an age-limit on grasping this concept either. Meaning is embedded into each of our vessels, and it doesn't expire until we do. The grace in that says it doesn't matter if you're five or sixty-five, there's always time to figure it out as long as you have air in your lungs. Everyone reaches their calling at different times anyway. Your calling isn't something you can compare. If you're not operating in it yet, it's because you only know what you know. Be confident in that and humble enough to evolve. Take the limits off yourself and accept that it will unfold inside of you if you seek it. Like a chocolate box covered in a wrap, it'll begin to come loose and expel every sweet gift inside. What you know will give you the courage to ignore the naysayers and doubters. You know, the people who say you're too young or too old to start doing x, y, and z. Their opinions don't hold water.

Purpose In Every Challenge

Every new opportunity challenges how you view yourself and how much you trust your purpose. At least, that's what I discovered nine and a half years ago. In June of 2010, one of my dearest friends asked me to plan her baby shower. I had just gotten my feet wet in event planning. Still, she trusted in my ability to put together an experience that would be described as opulent, perspective-shifting, and blissful.

Now, throwing a baby shower is enough pressure on its own. But this specific shower had a new level of weight that I still haven't experienced to this day. You see, my friend became pregnant after being raped. The incident not only momentarily stole a piece of her, but it implanted an unexpected seed. As a woman of faith, she battled with the idea of aborting or going full-term. Yet, she decided to do something I'm not sure if I would've even been able to handle. She chose to go full-term and decided to celebrate his life and raise him as if he was a child conceived out of love. The amount of trust that she had for me to be able to do this for her makes me speechless still. I was imparted with the duty of crafting a space that welcomed baby boy and made sure everyone knew that he was a king , no matter how he got to this earth. It was an honor, but it also forced me to go to war with imposter syndrome as a newbie. I knew I had to make this event top-tier to ensure my client was making the right decision by celebrating this new life. I praise God that this was my first official event because it made me step up and grow. It showed me that event planning isn't about me. It's always about the client! Of course, we say these words as service providers, but to live it and to believe it is different. I bloomed into a professional that was able to strip myself away from the project. That way, I could be the vessel used to bring special occasions together, thus providing my clients with an experience beyond their imaginations. It was one of the proudest moments in my career; the only thing that could top it would be Michelle Obama hiring me to work an event.

Challenges, no matter how big or small, push you into arenas to either war alongside your purpose, or against it. They teach you how to step inside your purpose and when to sit down and listen to it. I know my purpose is to bridge communities, induce healing, and create brave spaces. I'm lucky enough to do this via event planning and coaching. Whenever people ask how a field like this could be driven by purpose, I let them know that events are the glue that tethers souls residing in physical bodies together. They give us reason to commune, exchange emotions, and even create open portals for healing. The experiences we share when we set aside time to gather, even if it's just with ourselves, are why we run to spaces that welcome and nurture us. It's also the reason we pay others to design and host them. From birthday parties to retirement extravaganzas, the role of an event planner is to handcraft moments via tapping into the five senses and present them to attendees. This is why I put my heart and soul into each event, and I plan on showing you how to do the same. I know that every single second of an experience is worth more than gold, and should be treated as such. From the moment an attendee walks out of their car, to the smells upon entrance, all the way to final goodbyes, curators are tasked with stringing elements of joy, happiness, and gladness for each person in the room. The creation of these moments and more is what makes event planners necessities.

It takes authentic passion to dedicate yourself to handcrafting the vision of someone else. Working with people even when they're unclear about their desires requires mental toughness and fortitude. Without it, you'll be stuck between fleeting emotions that tell you when you feel like executing. Not to be rude, but we have enough professionals who operate on this level. What we need are service providers that do precisely this, they serve. They see the vision of their client and turn it into a masterpiece. This requires passion, dedication, and of course, being aware of your purpose. As I said earlier, my purpose isn't being an event planner, it's bridging communities and healing. My gifts allow me to use curating as the medium for executing my God-given mission. That's why I don't believe anybody can be anything. No, everybody has to be a master of themselves and aware of their mission, gifts, talents, and skills. This awareness produces a fire we call passion, and operating in these areas aligns you with your purpose. Without discipline to know thyself, you'll never be able to tap into what you do and why you do it.

That's why I designed my tagline the way I did. Being driven by purpose means my goal is always to encourage, edify, and take people on a journey to witness their own purpose. I remember what it was like to be voiceless…now you can't shut me up. Walking this way hasn't always been easy, but I promised myself I'd never go back to the darkness that plagued me. I'd fight like hell to never go back there. I live this out every single day by operating in my purpose at all times. I know and trust that some people are assigned to me. So much so, I believe you're one of them. I accept that I'm not for everybody, and everybody isn't for me, but you're still reading this because there's something pulling you to these pages. I don't take it lightly that you've entrusted me with empowering you and teaching you how to become a boss at event planning. I plan on continually pulling on your heartstrings and equipping you with the tools and resources I wish I had at the beginning of my career. I want to make this clear, though; I am not going to tell you what your purpose is. That's your job to discover. I know it ain't easy, but you have to care enough to want to listen in. This isn't your typical how-to book. At the time I'm penning this book, the world is in absolute shambles. Covid-19 has a tight grip, and racism is in full swing, but I stand as a believer that you can still be successful in the midst of this turmoil. The world hasn't stopped; we just have to pivot. With that said, we'll be covering a slew of event types, tools, and even what it means to host a successful virtual event.

I am grateful to have kept your attention for this long, and I'm blessed to be able to serve you in this way! If you have any questions throughout this read, please feel free to contact me on Instagram @CHBHevents or shoot me an email using info@ chbhevents.com.

More Than A Creative Outlet

A person's function is a key component of their purpose. By definition it can mean the following:

professional or official position: OCCUPATION
the action for which a person or thing is specially fitted or used or for which a thing exists: PURPOSE
Merriam-Webster

For this reason, it would behoove me to let you in on a secret you may or may not be privy to. I would recommend highlighting this next sentence. You, my friend, are an artist. I recognize the term art can be polarizing and potentially confusing. But here's why I'm letting you know who you are, artists are creators that take one medium and turn it into another. They are manipulators (only in the best and healthiest way). Essentially, art is the outcome of someone taking something and continually molding it until it fits the picture or sound they had in their minds. When you use this as your operational definition of an artist, then you can begin to undo the myths surrounding the function. I'm sure you grew up, like me, thinking artists were singers, dancers, performers, writers even. But cheers to a new understanding because you, my love, are exactly this. Before we get into the meat and potatoes of this book, I want to inspire you to accept this new title. Although I'm not in the business of convincing anybody of anything, I would like to emphasize a few things. Artists are not airheads, lazy, fluffy, or any other negative trope that's been given to us. We are master storytellers and experienced curators. Any idea you've had about artists prior to reading this section, I want you to erase it. We're starting over and redefining ourselves. The bad habits people have do not get to outline the function they're operating in; it only shows their personal flaws.

The next myth to bust is about money. The title artist is not synonymous with being broke. I understand the common story about artists is centered around them struggling to make a living for the sake of dedicating their all to their art. It's an amazing movie to watch, but this doesn't have to be your reality as you shift your paradigm of self and your functions. You can be paid and an artist without having to attain a level of celebrity. Most millionaires don't have public names, just big pockets.

The last misconception I'd like to address is focused on professionalism. Because people don't understand how to define artistry, they believe it's the polar opposite of business. As if being creative means you can't be business-savvy! Based on our jobs as event planners, I'd like to confirm that as a lie. You can be a visionary, a creator, and a successful CEO. Your function doesn't take away from your ability to turn a profit. If anything, it's your new secret weapon.

Tapping Into Your Talents

I'm excited about your journey because I'm reaping the rewards of my own. Learning to cultivate talents and giftings inside of myself has shown to be a profitable way of living. And I mean profitable in all areas, not just my bank statements. In recognizing what we're naturally capable of doing, we create a landscape that allows us to win a hell of a lot easier than forcing ourselves into molds we don't fit. Both the talent and the gift are one and the same. They co-exist as elements inside of us just waiting to be tapped into. They're such strong elements that they even travel through our DNA. Any time you see a family that is inherently great at the same thing, you realize it's deeper than them sharing the same skillset. That would assume they all had to acquire the talent, but we know they're born with it. There's something magnificent about structuring your thinking around talents and gifts like this. You can begin to unlock just how necessary and world-changing they truly are.

Since the creation of mankind, every human is born with something unique about them. I teach my clients that this purpose is so set apart that if they don't do it, it won't get done. Sure, someone else may have an idea that is 99% the same and execute on it. But that 1% of differentiation is a lot stronger than we give credit. That's the phenomenal part about writing this book. I know that no matter how much I give away, no one can plan events like me. This does not mean someone can't throw an event that's just as opulent, amazing, etc. It means that I'm Valerie Jenkins and there's no second version of me. My sauce, my flavor, my attitude, my zest, all of that can't be replicated. The same is true for you. You could tell me every step, for how you hosted an event, and I would get close, but I wouldn't be able to spark the same feelings as you. Being special has little to do with how different we are, and more to do with how much we emphasize those minute variations.

For those of you that are wondering why I still categorize ourselves as artists, I'd like to highlight a few key characteristics of event planners.

The basis of our gifting is attention to detail. We can see things that don't exist and experience them as if we were standing in the middle of it. All it takes is a few deep breaths, closed eyes, and then boom, we're living out an event being planned for the next year. It's as if our senses are stronger than most, allowing us to deeply feel our mental creations. We paint with our eyes closed and our hearts open. We construct images with colors that don't exist (yet) and layered details. You then look at our ability to manage the emotions of others, and you've got two characteristics that artists of other fields have. We guide our clients to what they really want versus what Pinterest told them they'd like. We provide spaces for these same people to commune and be themselves. This alone explains why we are just as artistic and necessary as sculptors, pianists, poets, etc. So no matter what you learned growing up, event planners are artists too.

On top of this, we tend to be empathetic people. For me, the space to empathize is critical for doing our work. Empathy is centered on emotional connection and events are about sparking certain feelings. The goal is to always create something that leaves your clients feeling good, in awe, confident, and aware. When you connect the two together, empathy plus your work, you make something that's absolutely tantalizing. You're essentially connecting with the person you're serving to be the vessel that manifests the feeling they're going after.

Early Beginnings

I'll never forget the first time I felt like an artist. But before I share that story, I want to give an example as to how things live through us before we even recognize them.

When I was in the fifth grade, I explicitly remember having the most tricked out lemonade stand on the block. I made sure customers were able to see us by bedazzling our sign, decorating the table, ensuring quality customer service, and more. Our stand was so successful that we'd bring it back every single year! People would be waiting for us to get our station ready and moving. Eventually, it was so successful that we turned it into a non-profit to serve Springfield Gardens Youth (S.G.Y.). I set-up every detail of this stand, and to think I couldn't see myself as an artist until I was a junior in high school is astounding.

What ended up occurring was a school presidential nomination and I was determined to win. I knew I was a worthy candidate, so I spent a crazy amount of time thinking of ways to show my diverse thinking and personality to the voters. After some time of plotting, I realized I would need to write a speech that caught the attention of my peers while also showcasing my abilities. The last thing I wanted to do was to step on stage and sound like every other class president we had. And just as easy as slicing a piece of warm butter, I ended up creating a mammogram for my name. The mammogram went as following: Victorious Authentic Loyal Effective Responsible Inspiring Energetic. Man, I can remember speaking in front of that crowd like it was yesterday. The energy I gave them was natural yet controlled, and they loved my creative twist on telling them who I am. With a presentation like that, it was of no surprise when I was elected class president. After spending a few moments to reflect on what I had done, I realized I was a creator. And although I ran away from my light for years after this realization, I knew an artist existed inside of me. Clearly, knowing it wasn't enough for me.

The difference between knowing and accepting is huge.

The moment I internalized my function for myself, I began to self-actualize my goals, impact, and clients' dreams. I understand this gift I have is God-given and it allows me to create the wow-factor for my clients. To be frank, I genuinely believe that to be true for you as well. But if you don't take the reins on this thing, you'll never be able to harness it in and control it. Seeing yourself as an artist is bigger than adding another cute title to your Instagram bio. It's about achieving a level of success you wouldn't have otherwise. It's about stepping into your purpose and daring the world to stop you. Because knowing more about your function, allows you to know more about yourself. And a self-aware event planner is an unstoppable one.

Now, let's get to planning your next event.

SECTION 2

Design

CHAPTER 1

Becoming A Co-Creator

The key to successful event planning is tapping into the personality of your client. You should know the person you're serving so well that you can discern the decisions they want to make before they even make them. Initially, this might sound impossible, but I can promise you'll start doing it naturally over time. The goal is to formulate a professional best-friend relationship. Here's what I mean, when you're incredibly close to someone, you can predict their behaviors. This understanding comes from listening, experience, and, most importantly, mutual communication.

It's the coupling of discernment and innovation that turns you into their co-creator, making them want to work with you for every event to follow. People need professionals like you to help manifest their internal desires into the earth. Trust, if they could do it without you, they would. So if you want to achieve a level of excellence, you have to learn how to train your mind into becoming the ingenious, artistic, and efficient version of theirs.

Imagine some of your favorite moments as a client. Without even knowing the specifics, I can bet you enjoyed the experience because you trusted them, they were able to do exactly what you wanted (even if you didn't specify in detail), and they felt like people you wanted to be around.

Picking The Right Clients

The first half of being a fantastic service-provider is picking the right clientele. Of course, you want your clients to live a dream and be the happiest they could be. But hear me when I say this, a happy client is the result of a happy service-provider. For example, when you enjoy the people or persons you're serving, you have a better attitude, energy, mindset and motivation. One thing I can't stand watching new entrepreneurs do is sell themselves short by taking on any and everyone for the sake of a check. You're way too talented to be working with people you imagine popping in the mouth every other client call.

I understand the hustle is real. sometimes you have to do what's needed, but this is the benefit of being your own boss. You make your own decisions. Not your family, friends, Instagram Direct Messages, or anything else.When you have a service or a product that's worth every dime, then you have the right to decline raggedy customers. Building your brand and clientele is based on strategy, not desperation. Read that again. Being desperate lets you undersell yourself, accept disrespect, bite off more than you can chew, and everything else that stresses you out, more than necessary.

Personally, I like to use a system to determine whether or not someone is a good fit for me. Here's a checklist I mentally use:

Potential Client Checklist

	Their character aligns with my spirit
	They're confident with being able to make payment
	Their personality allows me to do my job with few limitations
	They're excited about working with me
	They have challenging yet realistic expectations
	Their event doesn't explicitly go against my beliefs
	I have the tools, resources, and team members necessary for their event
	I have the time capacity to work with this person in this season
	This client doesn't have an extremely needy personality

If I'm able to check each of these off, I'm confident moving forward in our work relationship. You must have a checklist you use to decide who's for you and who's not. The moment you put a discovery call link on your website, email, social media, etc. you're opening the door for anyone to come in and request your services. With a checklist, you're able to swiftly determine whether or not someone will be a good fit for your company during the introductory Zoom or conference call. Feel free to use the checklist above or create one yourself. But regardless of which option you take, equip yourself with this as a resource. Every client you take on is a representation of your brand's mission, vision, and beliefs. If they counter any of these, you'll need to reevaluate your relationship. It might seem hard to turn down a client, but trust me when I say you'll be able to discern it. Your gut does not lie! Listen to it in your personal life, and also, most certainly in business.

I want to encourage you to use the referral system or self-blame while denying a client for my timid readers. For example, if you realize you're unwilling to work with someone, then look into your network of people that they might be better suited for. This way, you can give them a resource they need while relieving yourself of the job. But make sure you only send people that you genuinely believe could add value to your network. Don't be the person known for sending piss-poor referrals. That's a quick way to create a bad reputation in our industry. However, if you realize you're not connected to anyone you can vouch for, just let your client know upfront. This could look like sending the client an email that lets them know you either don't have the time or resources to create the event they're looking for, but you're grateful for their inquiry. This shouldn't feel like a lie if you simply don't want to work with them or because you don't have a good feeling. Your emotional capacity is a part of your resource bank! One thing I learned was to always be aware of how a project will impact my skills, my brand, my mind, my reputation, and my heart/spirit. If a client seems like they'll be emotionally taxing, you can either charge them an upcharge (aka an emotional tax that you'll factor into the overall cost for the service) or simply turn them away.

But let's say you come to realize that you genuinely can't do the proposed project. It's okay to let them know this too. We should always be open to taking on challenges, but these challenges shouldn't be so far outside of our scopes that we've failed before we even began. Use your discernment to decide what's a healthy challenge and what's a reach. Two ways to know is to review your resources and your time commitments. If you don't have the resources and/or don't have the time, the answer is simply no.

It's your business; therefore, it's your decision who you take on. Actually, let me rephrase that. You are the business! What did Jay-Z say? *I'm not a businessman; I'm a business, man.* Don't forget that in hard times. You reserve the right to refuse service, especially with those who don't know how to respect boundaries from the very beginning.

What makes you say yes to a client should be just as clear of a decision as no. I like to take on projects I've never done before. I like clients that make me go deeper and events that scare me but also excite me. Events that make me say, "I've been waiting on this opportunity," and will give me the satisfaction I need as a service provider. What'll make you say yes will probably be different from me, so make sure you talk to yourself about the things you'd like to experience out of every new project.

Getting Your Clients

Now, here's the fun part. Landing a new client is always an amazing experience! Getting them to reach out to you shouldn't be a headache, either. Truthfully, you only need a few tools to streamline this process.

Consistent Inquiries Checklist

	A website that includes • An about section. • Your mission statement. • A photo of yourself and your team (if you're working with one). • A contact page that has your city/state, an email, discovery call link, and a timeframe for when you'll respond (48 hours). • A contact form that's linked to your email. • A service page that outlines the kind of events you enjoy working • Testimonials - this can be a separate page or in the footer section of the other page. These are most effective with their name and photo.
	A discovery call link connected to your Instagram, website, and email signature. You can create a free one through Acuity. This allows you to create a calendar for clients to book their own calls based on a schedule that works for you.
	Your title in your social media name and bio (not username if you prefer to use your name).
	Website link in your social media bio connected to your services page. Please link this in your website section, not in the bio itself. It needs to be hyperlinked.
	An email in your social media bio/business page as a link.
	A professional email such as valerie@chbhevents.com.

Once you implement these and market yourself accordingly, you'll begin to receive appointments for introduction, aka discovery calls. Now, once you've received your bookings, it's your job to seal the deal.

Whenever I get on a new call with a potential client, I make sure I'm in a professional headspace. I affirm that I trust myself to lead this call and trust my skills. I speak with intent, and I remember that I am the brand. The product they're looking for exists inside of me, and I'm capable of determining whether or not they're a good fit for me. I go into a servant-leader's mind, and I focus on making the client as comfortable as possible. This is a major key. The more comfortable a prospective or potential client is, the better they are at communicating their needs and desires. I can't truly gauge if I'm the woman for the job if they don't give me all the information I need. So while on the call, I make sure I'm approachable, respectable, and understanding. I know different people go through other actions to prepare for a sales call, like setting the mood in their environment, wearing a specific kind of outfit, drinking tea, or even exercising. However, I enjoy preparing my mind and heart to be open to understand the needs of this individual. I tell my mind and ears to hear and listen to them as they speak. Even better is to prepare my eyes to watch their body language if we can do a Zoom call. Preparing my inner self gives me the competitive edge to be and feel confident externally on the call.

Pre-Call Preparation List

	Make sure you confirm the booking prior to the call.
	Send them an email with the call information if you don't use a program like Acuity to do it for you.
	Send an email the day of to confirm their attendance a second time.
	Research your client online to see their personality type (if you're able to find them online)
	Review the form they submitted to book the call. This form should ask what kind of service they're looking for, if they already have a budget in mind, when the event will potentially be, and the event type.
	Test your Zoom or conference call link an hour before the call.
	Hop onto the call five minutes before the client and turn on the recording function.

Once you're on the call with your prospect, you would've already established a level of professionalism with them just by using the tips above. The goal is for the client to trust you so you can serve them best. Above all, we're service providers. Emphasize this while you're on that initial call by encouraging them to ask you as many questions as they'd like during the allotted time. This gives you even more in-depth insight into what their personality type is and, of course, the job at hand. This information should never lead you to categorize your clients by their personalities, though. Everyone and every job will be different (even if certain elements seem similar). Going into every call, knowing you know nothing about this individual, encourages you to be a better listener instead of a desperate salesperson. The best salespeople understand that their job is to hear and understand the needs and then assess whether they can do this. I would also recommend not giving away pricing information on the first call. Leaving the money conversation out allows you to analyze what's being said without dollar signs racing your mind. After the call, you can then send them a professional quote within forty-eight hours (ideally twenty-four) through email. Make sure you let them know you'll be doing this once they ask about costs or during the budget conversation. Once you send the quote, you can also include a link for a follow-up call forty-eight hours (in the email with the bid) after they've received this email.

All in all, you just have to consistently show up as your best and reschedule if you absolutely can't (because life happens).

Becoming Their Co-Creator

At this point, not only have you had your discovery call and sent over your project quote, but you've received your deposit and signed your contracts! Congratulations on the abundance to come! More importantly, congratulations on the work that's ahead. Getting the client and determining whether or not they're for you is the relatively easy part. Once funds have been exchanged and NDA's have been signed, it's time to get to the nit and gritty and become their co-creator.

Honestly speaking, if you prioritize open communication, then this won't be a daunting task. It'll make you a bit nervous because you want to produce the event they wanted while also going above and beyond (while staying inside their budget). But these nerves are natural and shouldn't make you think you're incapable of performing. Here's what I like to do so I'm best able to serve my clients.

1. Video conference over phone calls. This allows you to read body language and see how your client is feeling.

2. Speak regularly. No matter where you are in the project, make sure you're communicating frequently.

3. Be available, but with boundaries. Let your clients know when they can reach you and be available when they do.

4. Respond quickly.

5. Research their ideas and provide them with tools to help them see their vision come to life.

6. Ask if they have any special days they'll be unavailable during your contract. Make them aware of yours as well.

7. Be efficient and effective with your work. Time is an extremely valuable resource, use it accordingly.

Your job is to create what's inside their minds while emphasizing the preconceived emotions they hold in their hearts. This is not your event. This is your service project. Keeping this frame of mind will make you one of the most sought after professionals no matter what industry you work in. Your ideas matter as long as they best-serve your client. Your creativity will flourish as you recognize the lines and boundaries inside of every work-relationship, and your clients will appreciate your end-products.

Pitching Yourself

Don't be afraid of pitching yourself to those who need your services. Yes, word of mouth will bring you customers, and so will your booking link, but pitching yourself helps you become a better salesperson. I know most people cringe at that word, but let's be honest here, that's what we are. If a sales exchange happens and you're the orchestrator of it, then you're a salesman. To get those testimonials and experience you need, I recommend pitching yourself consistently to one of three people.

1. Someone who doesn't know how to throw an event.

2. Someone who doesn't want to do it themselves.

3. Someone who doesn't want to spend the time doing it.

Observe your social media to see who has birthdays and anniversaries coming up. Reach out to them to see if they have someone who's helping them prepare for that event. Do this with the intent to serve and to learn, not to get rich. Obviously, you should charge accordingly, but the money is the least valuable resource you'll get out of this exchange. If you can pitch ten people a week, and land at least two of them every two weeks, think of the amount of information you'll receive by planning their events! You'll become a master in this industry and learn what kind of events you like best, your preferred locations and such. Once you know you've mastered being a creative, ever-evolving and learning, event planner, you'll never undersell and underestimate yourself again.

CHAPTER 2

My Secret Ingredients

D o you know what's beyond crazy to me? We have all of these top-tier planners in the world afraid of someone utilizing their methods and practically outdoing them. Obviously, I understand it from a traditional business perspective. You've spent countless hours of research and theory testing to create and streamline your processes. You took loss after loss to create enough momentum to generate your wins. Once you master a system that works for you, you'll fight tooth and nail to protect it. I get it. But looking back over the baseline of my career, I could have used so much more detailed insight to avoid some very obvious pitfalls.

Because of my journey as an entrepreneur, I don't come from the belief system of *touch the stove to know it's hot*. That's why my goal is to share every ingredient I have so you can learn how to create your own sauce without having to get burnt in the process. And trust me, I could care less if we use the exact same elements. We're all divinely talented. I personalize my measurements and execution towards my clients and my mission. So if I can share with you everything I know from A to Z in hopes of saving you from some unnecessary pitfalls, then that's precisely what I'm going to do.

First Things First

There is no event designing business without clients. Solving other people's needs is the center of what we do. With that said, this section will focus on what to do when you've officially signed a client agreement. I cover how to get clients in chapter six, so don't stress about this just yet. In the meantime, let's go over the first things I do after landing a new contract.

To start, I always make sure I make an outline of the client's needs. I want to know the event type, if they've attended a similar event, their goal for the attendees' experience, and specialty items they'll need (like a venue that's handicap accessible).Here's a list of questions you can use to guide this conversation (note, you should already know the client's budget before having this talk):

Why do you want to plan this event? Is there anything personal about this?

What's your overall goal for this event?

Do you have a system in place to measure whether or not this event was a success?

What are five things, or less, that this event must have?

What should this event absolutely not have?

What are your highest aspirations for this event?

What are your biggest fears for this event?

Do you have an inspiration board created?

Have you ever attended an event like this before? If so, what did you appreciate, and what did you hate about that experience?

Are you intending on purchasing event insurance?

Are there any dietary restrictions or allergies we need to know about for your attendees?

Will anyone be honored at this event?

Will there be an abundance of out of town guests?

Will you need event staff?

This list is created with the assumption that you've already asked your client when and where the event will occur. What their budget is. What the event type is. How many guests will be invited. If they have their venue secured already. Compiling a checklist based on the questions above will give you the plan you need to ensure you're keeping your client satisfied throughout the planning process. A bonus step I encourage you to partake in is looking at this needs assessment you've created and check for any resources to help make the event a reality. I especially like to think of any colleagues I can use as vendors, caterers and so forth. These can be florists, chefs, marketers, performers, anyone I know that can accomplish the job at hand. This is crucial because you're only as good as the people you partner with. Remember, people believe they've made a great decision based on their experience. Nothing tops an extraordinary experience as a client. Therefore, the companies you involve in projects should exemplify the same level of professionalism as yourself.

After taking the checklist into account and analyzing my resource/network bank, I then go into research mode. I look into the elements needed to create the event's theme, trigger individual senses and feelings, and ways to do all of it inside the designated budget. This is a pretty simple step, but it's just as important as the others for the creative process. Whatever my client wants to create more than likely has been executed before. To generate the inspiration I need, I love using search engines and even social media apps like Pinterest to look up various looks and ideas. Now, this should not be turned into a copycat spree. Getting insight into similar events should spark your mind into curating something new. It should never encourage you to produce a replica of someone else's hard work.

Event Phasing

After you understand the money you have to work with and the feelings your client wants you to generate, you can then get to work on phasing out your event. The capital and the feelings are precursors to this because the emotions determine how deep the event will be. The money outlines whether or not it'll be an Eiffel Tower or an Eiffel Tower-like experience. To know this and to design around this information will save you from many of the financial hardships I endured in my early years. To start, it'll save you from making promises that their budget can't keep. As we'll continue to cover throughout this book, being creative can motivate you to go above and beyond. Which is a fantastic quality to have if you're able to do so without going over budget. I vividly remember a time in my career when bills were crushing me, and I couldn't understand why. I was using my gifts, and I was astounding my clientele. Little did I realize that passion doesn't pay for anything. I was placing myself in predicaments that weren't necessary by doing work far more expensive than what the client could foot. I would look at the possibilities of an event and allow myself to dip into my own funds to finance a project that should've been funding me. I would spend every single penny on the event itself, forgetting I had to get paid too. Praise God, I'm not falling for that anymore. If they can't foot the bill, we can't do the work.

Now that that's clear, let's get to phasing.

This part of event planning is the core of everything you'll do. It's where you begin storytelling and hell, even prophesying about what's to come at your upcoming function. Depending on how detailed you are in this phase will determine how you're able to execute the event itself.

Programming

Like any musical, wedding, recital, or poetry slam, your event needs to have a program. To make it simple, there should be a play by play of moments to occur at your event that tell a story. When done correctly, the event itself should feel like a well-choreographed dance! Each step streamlining into the next, creating a fully felt movement that's equally understood by the audience.

The most significant part is that your dancers in this scenario are your guests and any live performers! What a program does is create an outline for them to move to while building anticipation and expectancy. That's the center of any good performance and event! The key to maximizing this is creating a crescendo effect within the event. Here's where your outline comes into play. To create hype, anticipation and excitement, you must stack your program in a way where each phase is more intense than the other. This doesn't matter if you're throwing a healing circle for mourning women or Diddy's next birthday party; you must master building excitement. The mountain top, aka climax of your program, should host the most dramatic part of the entire event.

For the program, I like to use these pillars for building outlines:

1a - Pre-Event Buzz

1b - Day of Anticipation

2 - Guest Arrival

2 - Start of Show

3a - Guest Acclimation

3b - Start of Show

4 - Halfway Mark

5 - The Climax

6 - Ending High

7 - Guest Departure

The first two pillars are based on marketing. Whether the client is doing it themselves or you're working with a marketing expert, they must be included in your programming. Most phenomenal events start by creating pre-event and day of buzz. No matter the channels being used to do so, it's imperative that the coming guests are thrilled guests. Mainly because it's a lot easier for someone to have an amazing time if they come with the expectation of doing so.

Before working on the next seven pillars, you must take into account how much time you have. How long is the venue letting you rent? Does this include set-up and breakdown time? If not, how much time are they allowing you to use? Is there any kind of rush for set-up or breakdown due to the event space having another event close in time? Get very clear on how many hours you have down to the minute.

The second pillar is the guest's arrival. I'm sure you've been to an event, and it could have been considered top tier, but the parking was a mess, and the entrance was underwhelming. Don't force your people to go through that kind of torment. Create a very clear roadmap for how parking will work, how many cars will be available, and if shuttles can be used. Then, ensure the parking lot itself doesn't look atrocious and use signs only when necessary. The feeling of luxury starts as soon as your guests' park, not when the showcase or festivities begin. The next part is to get creative with your entrance. What will your guests see, hear, smell, maybe even have the opportunity to taste? Where will their coats and hats go, potentially even shoes? How will they be sure that they're in the right location? All of this should fit within a ten-minute (thirty-minute maximum) timeline. Guest arrival is quick and fleeting, but it confirms whether they were right to have their excitement.

Once they've arrived and potentially removed any unnecessary clothing or received welcome bags, they immediately begin the guest acclimation phase. Now is the time to show them they belong at this event. Convince attendees they were thought of in the planning process. At a conference, this might include a quick moment to rally and get the attendees hype. For a holistic retreat, this might be time for everyone to sit and journal their expectations. Regardless, you want to create an environment that encourages guests to mingle before anything official occurs. While brainstorming this section, be sure to think of your introverts, ambiverts, and your extroverts. You'll also want to think of any pop culture events that might've impacted the attendees' community. Is this area known for anything? Was there any recent political turmoil? Have they experienced a major sporting win (or loss)? Pro-tip: check-in with a local, and search the location on Google to see what's been going on. Knowing this information makes you sensitive to the things they'll be sensitive to. This is especially important if the event isn't anything like a birthday party or wedding celebration. where most of the hosts and centers of attention are assumed to be locals. Essentially, what you're tapping into is tribalism, and we all take part in this phenomenon. There's a pride that comes from being from a place and knowing it well. We see comedians like Katt Williams use this during his stand-up by using local information as a part of his bid. By showing you're aware of someone's immediate area, you reveal that you care about their experience enough to customize it to them. Find ways to include this in your guest acclimation phase by incorporating local dishes as hors d'oeuvres or colors of a sports team, whatever goes best with your event goal, budget, and intended emotions to trigger.

Once your guest is acclimated, it's time to start the show. I realize I'm using performative terms to describe any kind of event, but it's a lot easier to create a program if you do so. At this portion of the outline, your creative juices should be flowing. You'll need to make a note of everything that needs to happen before the event is halfway over and how to stack this event to continue building that necessary excitement.

Just like your guest arrival stage, the halfway marker will make or break your event. At this point, your audience is likely beginning to experience some sort of fatigue (even if you're still building excitement). Depending on the length of the event, I recommend using this as a fueling session. Avoid putting people through hours of interaction or deep thought without giving them something to eat and drink. You mustn't let people burnout due to hunger, thirst, or just straight-up boredom. If the event isn't long enough to accommodate a meal, incorporate some free for all. At a party, this might mean giving people the option of getting a light re-freshment. At a conference, this halfway point could be provid-ed for lunch or a time to order food. For a retreat, this moment could look like self-reflection on the previous sessions and quiet time. However, this portion could simply be an announcement for what's to come for a shorter event. Put yourself in the attendees' shoes. Ask yourself what they will need to make it to the climax with a full tank of energy.

Speaking of, the climax is the stage for your outline. Note, this is not a singular event that constitutes the entire moment. Remember, your people will be coming back from the halfway point, and you'll want to re-acclimate them into the energy of the space. Afterward, you'll introduce them to the star-moment of the event. You can do this slowly by dropping hints of something important to come, or you can make it plain as day by putting it on their program cards. Whatever this moment is, make sure you set your guests up in a way they're inclined to give their full attention and cooperation. Remember, this has to be the most dramatic point of the entire spectacle. This is the time that should be most remembered, loved, cherished, and appreciated. It's the moment where they realize how everything came together to make this authentic experience occur. Whether it's a performance, a speech, a birthday cake, or a contest, understand what's needed to ensure the client, the guests, and your team are satisfied.

Upon the climax reaching its peak (no matter how long the finale is), you should prepare for the sixth pillar of ending high. If you conclude by the time people are tired of being in a space, then you've waited far too long to send them on their way. Always use this pillar to create a pattern that hints or explicitly states a near conclusion after the climax, so you're leaving their most recent memories of the event as the mountain top moment. This stage could look like a final hooray or an acknowledgment session. The goal is to stop building anticipation after the climax while maintaining the excitement of what you created. Likely, mingling will take place during this wrap-up.

Finally, you've reached your last stage, the guest departure. You want the attendees to leave as well as they came. Creating an exit plan is vital for this moment. You'll want to effectively communicate how to best leave the space, where they can share their memories, and a final word from the host. While designing this, ask yourself how many people will be leaving at once. Is there a way to organize their departure into waves? How will you respectfully encourage them to leave the premises after talking to their neighbors about the event, are there any shuttles and so forth

There you have it. You now have your core event stages and their respective outlines. At this point in the process, you'll proceed by looking over your ideas, making sure each moment flows into the next, and what kind of vendors and potential performers you'll need to bring in. Which brings us to our next phase, event layouts. However, this will take more than a few paragraphs to detail at length. I've reserved how for chapter three. In the meantime, I'd like to talk to you about mental preparation.

As you can see, there's a lot of mental work that goes into phasing out an event. Each stage has its own sub-stages stacked on top of each other to reach peak excitement, satisfaction, and appreciation. Because of this, I'd like to take off my teacher hat and put on my coaching hat for a moment. Like I tell the women I mentor, you must take care of yourself to take care of your work. You are worthy of this industry if you plan on giving it all you've got and granting yourself the freedom to try and try again. Although our final products seem glamorous, the work that goes into being an event planner is all but that. This is a skill based on strategy, chess, if you may. To help you start working your mental muscles in a way that sparks your creativity, I'd recommend trying out the following exercises.

1 - Put down your phone and start using a pen again.

There's something spectacular about slowing yourself down enough to write. It forces a level of thought that typing does not. Write as frequently as you can, whether on a whiteboard to save paper or in your favorite journal. Spend some time with your ideas and yourself.

2 - Write down ten ideas a day (or maybe even a week).

Since we're on the topic of ideas, I'd love for you to try this exercise. To do this, keep a notebook only to be used for this. They say a good idea comes to a dime a dozen, but if you learn how to generate more ideas more frequently, you're increasing your chances of developing something that'll be worth more than gold for you one day. Also, don't limit yourself to just event ideas here. Give yourself ten minutes and get to writing as many as you can think of. If you don't handle time pressures well, keep your list close to you and fill it out all day. To make sure these get used, I'd recommend reviewing them one to two times per month.

3 - Use social media effectively.

While scrolling through content, you could construct a feed where most of the content is used to inspire you. This could be for mental strength or event strategies, regardless; make social media work for you if you decide to engage with it. The next tip inside this section is to create bookmark folders for your saved Instagram posts. When you see content that makes you want to attend an event or replica a piece of it, save it! Don't be fooled and think you'll remember it because you're more than likely not going to, and that's okay.

<u>4 - Host your own events.</u>

You don't have to wait on landing a client to get better at using your skills. Look deep inside yourself, see what kind of event you'd love to associate with your company, and plan it. Size doesn't matter here; artistry does.

<u>5 - Test your theories!</u>

The final exercise I'll give you is to test the thoughts that you have. Again, this shouldn't be limited to our work! One way to become a better artist and strategist is to become the two in all areas of your life. Your health should feel like a dance. Your routine should feel like a play. Your thoughts should be backed by evidence. Testing to see results in all areas of your life will make you keener, more aware, more agile, and overall better at the things you do. It'll take real creativity to do this, and it'll be the start of a new journey, but the outcome will always be worth it.

***

I'm so glad to know you're moving through this book! I pray you take all the information in this chapter and selah on it before chapter three. This content was all about helping you learn how to get the information needed for phasing your event and how to turn it into a pre-, during-, and post-event program. Once you turn this page, we'll go more in-depth into how we make your outline come to life.

SECTION 3

Execution

CHAPTER 3

Crafting The Sauce

Have you ever bought a masterclass, or maybe even a webinar, and by the end of it you were left wondering how you were going to use the information? You invested all that time in getting to know the *what*, but you were left in the air in terms of the *how*? Trust me when I say, I've been there, done that. Typically this is done as a sales tactic to influence you to buy the coach's next offer. To be frank, it's a pretty successful tactic too (otherwise all of Instagram's gurus wouldn't be using it). However, I know how frustrating it is to get all amped up about the information, only to be left wondering what the heck you're supposed to do now.

That's why we'll be walking through various scenarios that give clear examples of how to weave together some of our secret ingredients from chapter two. That way you can take what you've learned and run with it.

The Boundaries of Freedom

Before we dive into the examples of how to use color, scents, and what you should and should not use for specific events, I want to talk about the boundaries that exist inside of artistic freedom. To start, let's go into some word definitions.

Ar·tis·tic | *adjective*

having or revealing natural creative skill;

aesthetically pleasing;

relating to or a characteristic of art or artistry

Oxford Dictionary definition

Free·dom | *noun*

the power or right to act, speak, or think as one wants without hindrance or restraint;

the state of not being imprisoned...

Oxford Dictionary definition

I like to think of artistic freedom as the power of revealing your natural creative skill that is aesthetically pleasing without restraint. In short, it's being able to express your innate creativity without limits. For ourselves, the only boundary from letting this definition reign true would be ourselves. But in business, those boundaries rightfully exist with each client we take on. Do you remember when we addressed the importance of client comfortability? Well, here's the summary of that piece. Creative aka artistic freedom is built as you cultivate your relationship with said client.

It's a privilege that's executed upon the comfort of your client with you, the service provider. The equation is quite simple.

The more comfortable they are with you = The more freedom you have as their planner.

If not for any other reason, you should fight hard to ensure your client's trust in you thus comfortability. Restriction can cause you to think outside the box, but it can also stifle you. So, the less restrictive your client is, the better you're able to create, and the better you're able to serve them. Note, this restriction has less to do with the budget and far more to do with your ability to ideate the event itself. As an emphasis on previous chapters, keep this in mind while pitching to clients and letting potentials reach out to you. If they don't feel right, more than likely; it won't go right. Gratefully, I can count on one hand, maybe three times, when I wasn't able to creatively flow. I knew from the beginning they weren't the client for me, but I told myself it wouldn't be that bad to take on their project. Take it from me, it will be that bad, if not worse. Taking your time to let your client evaluate you whilst you do the same is paramount for your longevity.

Your Secret Weapons

Now for the juicy information, tea if you will. How do you craft the feelings you want to spark during your events? The answer seems simple, but oh, it's complex. At its core, triggering emotions is based on curating the perfect setting dependent upon the client's needs and the crowd's demographics. The data you'll need to begin include: age range, gender(s), race(s) and culture(s) The remaining demographics will be based on nuances such as potential language barriers, disability access and so forth. Allow this information to fuel how your event is set-up i.e.: floor plans, food groups, the flow of movement, flower type, staffing needs, and more.

Once you begin the phase of considering decorations, your focus should go towards colors. This is where things get fun and in a sense, layered. Although I have several years of experience in the advice I'll be sharing, I decided to read up on several articles to learn more about the emotional connection to colors. The two main articles I'll be using outside of my personal expertise come from *Psychology Today*[1] and other online resources[2]. All of these articles can be seen in the footer of this page. Let's begin our lesson on colors.

Saturation and Brightness

There's a high likelihood that you've tried to edit a photo before. If so, then you're familiar with saturation and brightness being two tools you use to alter an image. How many of us know their definitions and functions? For starters, saturation is the purity and

---

1 https://www.psychologytoday.com/us/blog/people-places-and-things/201504/the-surprising-effect-color-your-mind-and-mood
https://www.psychologytoday.com/us/blog/people-places-and-things/202009/science-based-color-selections
https://www.psychologytoday.com/us/blog/people-places-and-things/202005/pick-green-almost-any-green

2 https://www.webmd.com/balance/ss/slideshow-colors-affect-you
https://www.verywellmind.com/color-psychology-2795824
https://99designs.com/blog/tips/how-color-impacts-emotions-and-behaviors/

even intensity of a color. You know how you can shift the color of an image to appear grayer by removing saturation or enhance the colors that exist by increasing it? This scale represents how pure a color is. Any color that isn't mixed with white or black is considered to be pure. You can measure its saturation by seeing how bright it appears next to white and black surfaces (neither should dilute the brightness). So for example, electric red is far more saturated than powder blush. You can imagine how different someone would feel walking a room with powder blush decorations versus electric reds. The expectations of what's to occur in such a space shift just as their emotions would.

Next is brightness.

Just like bulbs, brightness in color is associated with how light it appears to be. An example I'll use here is neon pink versus forest green. The neon pink, whether you place it next to white or black, is going to be very bright. While the forest green is going to be dimmer in appearance. This matters because the brightness of the colors you use for an event will set the tone! *Psychology Today* gives an example of how less saturated yet bright colors are more relaxing (bright sage green) while the more saturated and dimmer colors are more energizing (sapphire green). Make sure you don't confuse dim with gray! A color can be dim while also being very saturated like deep burgundies.

To make this section easier to apply, all you need to do is ask yourself, '*At the base, am I trying to get people hype or calm them down during this event* (or maybe even event phase)?' By sticking with the formula of energy = more saturation, less brightness, and calming = less saturation, more brightness, then you're on to an amazing start.

Warm and Cool Tones

Moving on, we'll be shifting our focus to tone. Just like our seasons, colors can be categorized into two categories: warm and cool. Our warmer colors are made up of colors like reds and oranges (sometimes yellow). Our cooler colors are blues and greens. The reason why this category uses words that remind us of the weather is due to colors being able to influence our perception of temperature. For example, in places where cooler colors are used, we perceive the place to also be cooler, while expecting the opposite with warmer colors. A great pro-tip here is to use this to your advantage if your event is being held in a location that has extreme weather on either side (hot or cold).

In general, those that have studied emotional responses to colors have noticed that we're drawn to warmer colors. This makes them amazing tools while trying to highlight a centerpiece, aka focal point (or space) of an event. They even mention people finding themselves more attracted to people seen around warmer colors compared to cooler tones. They also seem to be friendlier. Skin tone plays a huge role in this as well. Never, and I mean never, make the mistake a major network for Black people did when they hosted an awards ceremony with blue carpet. Large amounts of blue flooring and darker skin clash almost every time, as the blue will make the skin appear to be ashy; even if it's not. I know this is probably a lot to take in, but trust me when I say, it's worth the study. We live in a colorful world, and learning how to utilize it will set you apart like none other. Figure out your color theme and layer it up! Also, give yourself grace. Learn the basics and have fun with it! At the end of the day, if your client is happy, then that's your focus. If three of the guests complain about the colors based on their own experiences with it, don't stress yourself out.

Color Profiles

Again, I'm all about practicality. Use this section as your individual color code.

<u>Red</u>

Seen as a color of strength, passion, and energy. Chromotherapy uses the color red to increase circulation in the body for patients and stimulate the mind. This color is known for encouraging people to respond quicker and with more assertion. These benefits make this perfect for mature events, hype events, and athletic events based on strength (like weightlifting). However, it's terrible for settings and events that require strategizing and analytical thinking. Studies have shown that our ability to think is hindered when under the influence of this color. So if you're doing something for the office or teaching a creative skill, avoid using it. Red has also been linked with amplifying negative emotions like failure and danger when used in excess and even triggering migraines.

<u>Yellow</u>

Crazy enough, this is the least liked color of them all (especially yellow-green). But if used in moderation, it can trigger feelings of happiness and spontaneity. In healing practices, it's believed to stimulate the nerves and body. It's also great near food as it's a warm color and stimulates the appetite. But if used in excess, the amount of light it reflects can cause mental strain.

Purple

Ah, the color of royalty. Honestly, it's my favorite. Purples are used to spark creativity, sensuality, and more. It's connected with being of higher status and riches, and even divine rights and practices. Next, it's seen as a mysterious color and luxurious. Like blue, it's great for health and beauty themes.

Blue

If you're stuck with no immediate ideas, think of the color blue. It's known to be the most well-liked and received color. It's been seen as a color that helps our behavioral patterns and even rewires our circadian rhythms. It's associated with water, beauty, health, and even security. This is due to us feeling safer when influenced by this color. We also tend to feel more relaxed. For these reasons, we have a higher sense of trustworthiness with it too. The site 99 Designs gives the example of darker blues being great for corporate while lighter blues spark friendlier feelings. Think of popular social sites like Dropbox and Twitter here. In chromotherapy, it's used to soothe illnesses and even treat pain. On the downside, it's also seen to spark migraines as well.

Gray

There's no color more professional than this one. It's formal, serious, and responsible. Which is perfect for executive meetings, not so much for baby showers. Its old-fashioned nature can be seen as too conservative and emotionless. When designing non-corporate events, it doesn't mean you should avoid the color altogether. Like every other neutral color, it has its usage.

White

As minimalism is still trending, white is its perfect color. It's seen as chic, clean, refreshing, opening, and simple. To bring balance into your designs, white can be useful for connecting all of your elements. Typically it's also used to spark positive emotions, and we're better able to read each other's facial expressions. But, you must be aware of the cultures attending your event. In the east (to be more specific, t East Asian), white can be used for mourning the way we use black in the west.

Pink

Who doesn't think of *Legally Blonde* or *Mean Girls* when we talk about the color pink? Known for femininity and softness, pink is a classic. It shouldn't be limited to the two though (although also amazing for sparking feelings of romance). Pink knows no gender boundaries. So aside from femininity, it's also used for charm, sweetness, and cuteness. It encourages sensitivity and even caring.

Brown

The most natural color you could ever see, popularly being used to showcase the liveliness of earth and being *au naturale* . A common feeling that arises by seeing this color is even-temperament, while on the contrary, it's also connected to being old-fashioned and dependable.

Black

When I think of power, the color black pops up. It's associated with being sleek, classic, and even modern. Like its opposite, white, it's also simple and neutral. Known for its professional look plus the ability to add sophistication and mystery to nearly anything, black is all around amazing. Like everything else that's good, though, in excess, it's too much.

Green

Blue may be the majority of people's favorites, but green is the most diversely used. It's great to spark creative thinking, be encouraged to remember positive emotions and memories, keep a healthy mindset, feelings of happiness, feeling clean, social responsibility and analytical thinking. Unlike pretty much every other color, green helps migraines calm down rather than amplify them. Also unlike other colors, green's only true negative outcome is based on personal perception! It's pretty much the holy grail of color.

Orange

If you're working an event and you want your attendees to feel strengthened and inspired, orange is your color. It's warm, so it's inviting and great to highlight the food at the event. It also makes people think of the fall months, and of course, Thanksgiving.

And that's all I have! Understanding colors shouldn't end here. This information is only the start, the real work is you going out and putting it to the test. I'll challenge you with creating a color palette for each of these scenarios:

35th birthday party | celebratory and 90s themed

Retirement party | Senior level executive, in-office

Tech conference | Millennial-focused, in-hotel, interactive

Bridal party | Emotionally-moving and fun

Anniversary party | Grown, romantic, celebratory

Bakery launch | Big city, anticipatory

Networking events | For entrepreneurs in hair care

Triggering The Other Senses

The emotional responses you want to ensue aren't limited to
the colors your attendees see. Colors do, however, influence
every other decorative decision that will be made to some
degree. Adding depth to space will require you to shape its
scents, tastes, and sights. Color could determine the scents,
if the candles will be seen. If not, then your scent isn't influenced by the totality of color as much as it would be influenced by the tone of the event. Your foods, on the other hand,
still get some of the influence of color. Convenience and rel-
evancy are absolutely greater determinants of food type, but
after this, how the food will be presented is next. Pro-tip,
people eat far more when the color of the food is similar to
the color of their plates. If you're wanting to slim the portions, put opposites on top of each other, like red curry on a
white plate. Next, you must pick out the sights. Will there be
art? Are there performers? What are the performers wearing?

Should there be a dress code? Will you have centerpieces? As humans we're complex and we enjoy well put together events. By tapping into the senses of your audience, you'll be accessing their emotions in a way that brings them to the desired and highly anticipated outcome they came for.

CHAPTER 4

The Fruits of A Successful Event Planner

Before we begin today's teaching, I'd like to emphasize that this section should be read slowly, and repeatedly. For the next few pages, we won't be covering what you should be doing as an event planner. Instead, we'll be outlining who you need to be as a successful one.

Growing up, I can remember the emphasis placed on us as children to know the fruits of the Spirit. I'm sure you've heard of them or even know the jingle, but if not, I'll list the verse here.

But the fruit of the Spirit is love, joy, peace, longsuffering,
gentleness, goodness, faith, meekness, temperance:
against such, there is no law.

Galatians 5:22-23

To this day, these fruits have proven to help us when loving ourselves and our neighbors. There is no fault in following these ways and they breed peace. In an effort to teach you about the characteristics you must have as a business owner, I'd like to use the same layout of these verses. Meaning, I want you to start thinking of your personality traits, habits, and characteristics as fruits. There's a saying that goes, '*The fruit will always snitch on the tree.*' I won't lie and say I know who coined the phrase because I don't. However, its sentiment is clever. I can tell what kind of person you are by the outcome of your fruits. And like an old wise man once said, good fruit doesn't come from bad trees.

To repeat, you must take your time to reflect while reading through today's content. You can know what to do and even how to do it, but if no one respects you while you're doing it, then it's pointless. Event planning is a service-based business. That means your sole purpose is to serve someone else's vision. If you can't harness the right attitude, you'll fall by the wayside of bad reviews, grouchy clients, and eventually a run down business.

With this explained, I want to present to you the fruits of a successful event planner.

They are as follows, patience, adaptability, innovation, attention, self-control, and consistency. These six fruits are your roadmap to success because each of them will require self-awareness and consistent self-assessment. And although not nearly as encompassing as the fruits of the Spirit, these will give you the fighting chance you need in this business. Let's move forward with breaking each of these down.

Patience

Contrary to popular belief, patience is not your ability to play the waiting game while twiddling your thumbs. Especially not in business! Patience is your ability to give every moment the time it needs to mature while doing all you can to nurture it. This is very different than sitting on the bench and hoping someone's going to sub you into the game. There's a level of assertiveness that comes with patience. A hint of perseverance, if I may. When we look at wildly successful people, they all had to wait on their moments by refusing to stop going after them. If you look at patience, it's a sequence of making moves until one of them finally reaches your intended destination. You don't force yourself to rush any of them and you don't take shortcuts. You take strategic action and watch every no morph into your yes. This requires deep-thought and yes, organization. The better your plan is, and the more willing you are to persevere even if a piece fails, the better you will be at being patient.

For your client, this will be a huge comforter for them. Everyone wants to feel like their service provider is taking their time to craft their idea and vision. Watching you give them grace for new ideas, potential changes in direction, and even potential redos (as many as the contract allows), grants them permission to be at peace.

And just a last-minute tip on becoming patient: however long you think something is going to take, multiply that times two.

Adaptability

If you want to be widely successful for several years, if not decades, learn how to adapt. By definition, it's the ability to make something suitable for a new use or purpose, or to modify. On a micro level, this could look like repurposing an old glass jar to use as a centerpiece decoration. But on a macro level, this skill is the difference between sinking and swimming during last-minute challenges that seem unconquerable. Knowing how to adapt, aka how to pivot, rests in your ability to assess your environment, potential threats, knowing your audience, foreseen challenges, multiple outcomes, and what the overall goal is. Remember when I encouraged you to work on your ideation skills by writing down ten ideas a day or week? This is where that skill comes into play. Once you finalize your assessment of the circumstance, you must come up with an idea (plan) to solve the problem.

Think about the year 2020. For our entire planet, major shifts happened. In 365 days, we experienced the Amazon rainforest catching on fire, COVID-19 forcing us to socially distance, Donald Trump losing the second-term presidency, SARS protests erupted in Nigeria, and so much more chaos that required us all to change focus. Out of them all, the coronavirus was the one that broke our industry's norms the most. I'm sure some of you felt it. You were planning an event for one hundred attendees, a deposit finalized, and out of nowhere, we weren't able to gather with more than ten people at a time. Our cities went on lockdown, curfews were implemented, even grocery stores had limits, and going outside required mask protection. It was apocalyptic, and many event planners lost their businesses. That is, until the Phoenix arose.

Online events have been on the rise for a few years now. But when our backs hit the corner after being pushed by venues closing and deposits not returning, we took them to a whole new level. Events limited to seventy seats were now hosting online conferences with five hundred attendees! DJ's took to live streaming platforms to give us pop artist battles, and nightclub feels in our living rooms. Graduations were on Zoom. Knowing how to pivot in the middle of a pandemic not only saved careers, but it kick-started joy! That's the outcome of making your circumstances work *for* you. You giving up because you can't adjust not only hampers your money, but it keeps you away from those you were intended to serve.

Remember, it's your job to create a Cinderella story no matter what. Not only that, you have the capacity to do so! Problems you weren't prepared for shouldn't keep you from being successful! They may delay you, they may require lots of shifts, but hunny, these problems can't stop you if you don't allow them to overcome your mind.

So adjust, and adjust as fast as you can while remaining effective. Your career depends on it.

Innovation

A man by the name of Abu Fofanah said on an online post, 'Don't reinvent the wheel, change the screws.' As someone that's helped over 100,000 women (mainly Black women) increase their sales, and the CEO of a multi-million dollar company himself, I trust the content. When we overcomplicate the process (any process), we find ourselves trying to outsmart systems that end up out-smarting us.

Working harder isn't innovation. To be seen as an innovator, you have to produce results, and market research will show you the successful wheels that already exist! Your job is to figure out why they work and what you can change about them to better serve your audience. Innovation is all about solving problems! But stressing yourself out because you want to start from scratch when research shows you what to do, is intentionally omitting sound reason. So use that natural attention to detail that you have and use it to study, research, and test! See what others have not (or haven't acted upon) and create the perfect masterpiece.

Ask yourself how you're creating innovative strategies for your branding, marketing, income, and event execution. Who has a similar audience as you? What are some ways people are catering to their clients? What are popular event decor ideas? This skill is all about asking the right questions and piecing the puzzle pieces together. My advice here would be to google innovative people and read up on why their ideas were considered so innovative.

Self-Control

Do what you say you're going to do. As an artist, we can get side-swiped by our ideas. Every day it's a new way to do x, y, and z. Every moment we find ways to build our portfolios and serve our people. It's easy to get tossed around by your own minds. Yet, the very same thing that keeps you ahead of competitors (your way of thinking) can get you behind in business. Here's what I mean. If you do not control your controllables, the moments that you can't control will impact your business (severely).

Examples of things we cannot control: receiving news of any kind, death, new life, acts of nature, catastrophic events, and world-changing moments. What we can control (assuming the mind is operating from a healthy place): our reactions, our organization, our workloads (entrepreneurs), belief patterns, philosophies, understanding of topics, and scheduling (again, entrepreneurs). Self-control (in all areas) helps give you grace when life happens and you must make adjustments.

But more importantly, self-control is about your health and the health of those around you. There are three universal truths: you are happening to yourself, life is happening to you, and you are happening to others. Controlling what you do has a direct impact on our responses in life and how we engage with others. Understand what you need to be your best, fuel yourself with those things, set boundaries for yourself, and honor them. Then repeat this process when working with clients, engaging with loved ones, and any other person you come into contact with.

Consistency

Stick with anything, and you'll reap results. And I mean that literally. As a coach, I hear people tell me how they're unable to be consistent with their goals, and I can't disagree more. All of us are creatures of habit. Some are just consistently inconsistent. You read that right, consistently *inconsistent*. So many of us have been trained to make decisions based on emotionalism that we're like leaves in the wind. Gone every which way because of how we feel in a moment.

The greatest indicator of what we're constantly doing is by analyzing our fruits. Sparse funds and incomplete ideas are two of the best ways to know that our energy isn't being well spent. Ask yourself, what are you dedicated to the most? Is it your growth, Instagram, your marriage, unhealthy eating, bad excuses, your hair - what is it? When people describe what you're known for, what do they say? Being aware of what your habits are will help you shift towards better habits for tomorrow.

Next, give yourself grace! For goodness sake, this is a new habit you're building. Don't go overboard and try being consistent with four new behavioral patterns. Pick one, get good at it (really good), and add to it. My recommendation would be to start off with your time. Becoming consistent with staying on time gives your remaining habits a foundation to thrive on. Lastly, don't think you're starting over when you fall off once or twice. This thing called life is cyclic. Don't beat yourself up because you had a relapse, just hop back on and keep moving forward. Punishing yourself is pointless. Read that again if you have to. Punishing yourself not only takes up time, but it stacks negative emotions that go against our self-worth, esteem, and confidence. So no matter how many times you have to try again, keep doing it.

***

I pray that these words have helped you ask deeper questions about your character. Bitesize success isn't our goal, longevity is. And the better you are as a human, the longer you can use your talents to make room for you.

SECTION 4

The Follow-Up

CHAPTER 5

Tweaking Your Style

Following up is the key that so many people forget to use after completing a project. Typically, we get so caught up in the highs of landing a client, fulfilling the project, and repeating that we neglect to set our eyes on reflection. Imagine how it looks from the lens of the client when you've invested all this time into working with a professional, giving them your money and finishing the project; all to look up, and never hear from them again after the event. They're left with zero opportunity to provide critical feedback, raving reviews that come from the heart, or an option to personally thank you. Ghosting your client because a contract is concluded can leave a weird taste in their mouths, and even skew how they saw the work you completed. Always, and in all ways, create space for every client to give you the outstanding, the good, the mediocre, and the ugly about their time working with you. Listen with a clear heart, ears, and mind. And no matter how much you may want to take offense, you must be mature enough to know the only way you can improve your business, is by listening to critique.

Every End Is A New Beginning

Following up is divided into two sub-categories. The first focuses on obtaining client feedback after a recently concluded project. The second is all about client retention. Both affect your bottom line in major ways! Before getting into the details, I want to highlight how each of these tasks can only be accomplished when you understand the cycles of business.

With every exchange, whether product-based or service-based, there's a sequence of introductions, a start, a conclusion, and a sequence of follow-ups. This flow of interactions gives a high-level overview of the phases of a contract. Remember this flow as you continue reading this chapter.

Let's get into the first sub-category: immediate client feedback.

Throughout the course of your project, you should be checking in with your client to gauge how they're feeling. Are they emotionally relating to what they're seeing? Does this look like the event they were trying to create? Do they feel seen, heard, and cared for? Although focusing on the post-contract follow-up, this shouldn't be the first time you ask your client for their thoughts. It especially shouldn't be the first time you ask how you're doing in their eyes. This way, upon reaching the final hoorah, you can look at the trend of their responses.

Think about it like this. If your client is only 'kind of' enjoying your work, but after the event is concluded they're astounded by how everything came together, you can compare their final response to their responses over time. What did you shift that made them happier? What are some elements they couldn't picture until the event? How did you work on your skills to better serve them? These kinds of questions should tell a story of how you satisfied a dissatisfied client. On the other hand, if your responses from the client have been phenomenal, and they give you a poor rating due to event-day mishaps, you can also use this to track what went wrong and how you lost their satisfaction. Now of course, there's the option of receiving fantastic feedback during the creation phase and after the event itself. You can use this constant feedback as a source of wisdom as well. What did they rave about? How were they impressed? What moments did they absolutely love?

So how should you follow-up? I'm glad you asked (by reading that sentence). The same way you should have a pitching template, you should also create a follow-up template. What I like to personally do is:

First - review the contract again by myself.

Second - hop on a call with the client before the final payment and re-review the contract.

Third - ensure the contract agreement is being fulfilled.

Fourth - twenty-four hours after the event concludes, shoot a thank you email asking for a review and/or for them to fill out a survey.

Fifth - store their review in a google document called *reviews* to be later used as marketing material and as a way to track my growth. Testimonials will be a huge determining factor as to how many new clients you're able to take on. For me, 90% of my work comes from leveraging testimonials.

0006774755

Sell your books at
sellbackyourBook.com!
Go to sellbackyourBook.com
and get an instant price
quote. We even pay the
shipping - see what your old
books are worth today!

Sixth (optional) - review their survey input.

Seventh - thank them for giving you their feedback and for allowing you to serve them in this way.

Bonus - having a gift sent for them to receive close to the time of the event's conclusion as a thank you. Of course, you can also just hand-deliver this at the event itself.

Honestly, following-up is extremely simple when you care about being an effective servant. To make your email useful though, you'll want to ask specific questions instead of just saying, *How did I do* in your email. If anything, you inquire on these outcomes:

Did I perform at the level you hired me for?

Did I create what you envisioned?

What did your guests think of the event?

Did we accomplish your intended goal for this event?

Do you feel satisfied now that the event is over?

If I could improve one thing, what would it be?

What did you absolutely love about working with me?

Asking every client you work with the same questions allows you to collect data on your services. Obviously you can ask way more questions than I supplied, but these will give you a well-rounded look into the customer's experience. Pro-tip, if you haven't asked in-depth questions with your previous clients, take the time to reach out to them and learn what you can. Even though their answers won't be fresh, you'll still be able to get a better understanding of your skillset.

***

Now let's cover the second sub-category: client retention.

The primary goal of following-up with an old client is to increase your rate of returning customers. As you do this, your flow of income becomes more predictable, your availability for the season becomes more clear, and you can anticipate client needs easier because you've worked with them before. Fortune 500 companies do this all the time! The understanding is this, it's a lot easier to get someone that loved your work to rehire you than it is to convert a stranger who doesn't know you from Adam. Both require nurturing, but one is far more willing to invest in you because they trust their return on investment (ROI) will yield high results.

However, this should not feel corny and cheesy. This phase of following-up will be continual and will require a systematic approach. This is where you get to flex your, "I told you I cared" muscles and truly mean it. Here's what I mean. If your client has a birthday, anniversary, business launch, or any special date they mentioned during your tenure together, reach out to them on that date! See, every follow-up shouldn't be business-related. At some point, you must care about the genuine well-being of your clients and take their life changes into account. You have no idea just how far sending love will take you. Aside from these types of follow-ups, there are referrals and repeats. Here's a scheduling example and definitions for each.

Date	Type	Action
Birthdate:	Celebratory	Send a gift to them like a Target gift card to their email.
3 months post-contract	Referral ask	Ask if they know anyone they'd be willing to refer me to for upcoming projects. Follow-up with them a week to two weeks later, if they say yes.
6 months post-contract	Repeat ask	Ask if they'd want to consider hiring you again for an upcoming event. Potentially send over a pitch to explain how you two could elevate the previous event you worked on.
1-year post-contract	Well-being check-in	Send an encouraging message (from the heart) to keep them inspired. Attach relevant resources like articles about their industry.

Repeat year	Well-being check-in, repeat and referral asks	Every year after your first year, you'll want to check-in at least once to let them know you're still looking out for them and would love to serve them, or someone they know again. This can be for their birthday or a year to the date of your last well-being check-in. This yearly phase officially kicks off on year two. Best if done via a video call.

This is an example of a system that works! When done correctly these follow-ups will keep you at the forefront of their event planning needs. I know it seems like a lot to remember, but if you go ahead and plan for it, all you'll need to do is the actual follow-up when the time comes around. Matter of fact, I trust this system will increase your client retention so much that I want you to try it out and send me your testimonials! You can send them to me at info@chbhevents.com.

It's All For Your Good

No matter what kind of feedback you receive from clients, remember it'll all be used for your good. You see, there's a philosophy that encourages us to take the boos and praises with a grain of salt. That is to not let yourself (specifically your self-worth and value) become defined by the words of others, and to instead focus on the simple truths found in each. Thus, if you get feedback that feels like a personal jab - take it, chew it, and spit out the bones. If you receive feedback that makes you feel like you're at the top of your game; take it; chew it, and spit out the bones. Allowing ourselves to become deflated or inflated from feedback is a dangerous game. Your one and only goal should be gaining new information to close your business's breaches. So never forget that feedback isn't personal, it's structural. Its sole purpose is to create a stronger foundation for you! And as you become more comfortable with asking for it, the better you'll become at separating your business from yourself.

SECTION 5

Business Foundations

CHAPTER 6

Separating The Art From The Business

The notorious line, *"I'm an artist and I'm sensitive about my…"* is a mantra that artists from every industry can relate to. Our ability to turn mere ideas into physical masterpieces requires emotional work in conjunction with being business savvy, skilled, and poised. Our strongest desire is for our audiences, aka clients, to feel what we feel, see what we see, and learn what we learned in the process of creating. It's a livelihood of pouring out so we can pour within each other. This is the great sacrifice of being artistic, but it's also our greatest reward. Even still, there must come a time when every artist takes off their Creative Enthusiast hat and replaces it with Chief Executive Officer or Founder. This time, although it can feel brutal, is the difference between a struggling artist and a thriving one. The kind of artist that sees the fruits of their labors while yet alive. Not the kind who's legacy wasn't honored until death.

The moment for this change isn't a singular event. It will occur throughout the ebbs and flows of every contract you land, project your sign and partnership you take on. In an instant, you'll go from analyzing the feel of a project to seeing if that feeling your creating is staying within budget. There are the moments when you must care about your company's profits and losses as much as you care about the creative outcome of the event. This isn't about limiting your creative ability. It's about honing in on separating the art from the business. Inevitably becoming a tool you use for building your brand, sustaining your business, and eventually scaling.

I'm sure from your own experience you recognize artistry as the emotional connection to the process of creation. While being a business owner is ultimately respecting the bottom line of every project. On a scientific level, these two skills utilize different portions of the brain, making them contrast greatly. This is why you can become more skilled in your art without it influencing your business skills at all and vice versa. With that being said, it's still very possible to become great at both. They don't compete with each other, they simply exist in different worlds. Understanding this, and knowing that you're both the artist and the owner of a business, is your ultimate key to success. Unlearn the myths that say you must compromise art or business to remain morally sound and respected. Let go of the celebrity examples of those who failed themselves by forgetting their ultimate missions. You, my friend, can and will have both the freedom of total expression and the security of a sound income in entrepreneurship. You'll begin this journey by defining what it means to be loyal to yourself and your client.

Loyalty As A Measure Of Success

In nature, there are three forms of connections called parasitism, commensalism, and mutualism. Parasitism occurs when one creature is using another for its own benefit and is simultaneously harming them. Commensalism exists when one creature needs another for its survival and it causes no harm to the other. Lastly, and the most beneficial, is mutualism. This connection is created when two creatures come together in need and mutually benefit each other. Neither party is harmed, and no one feels like they've been cheated. In business, our goal is to create mutually beneficial partnerships! Yet, so often, I'm told stories of women that ended up being the victim of a parasitic business opportunity because they had no idea what it meant to be loyal to themselves. Matter of fact, they had no idea how to define loyalty. So at this moment, I want us to cover the basics. What does it mean to be loyal?

For me, loyalty is the ability to set honest expectations of oneself and others, and doing exactly what I promised (whether to myself or other people). The reason I begin this definition with honest expectations is this… I cannot promise myself or anyone else anything if I'm not aware of my current capacity. If I tell myself that I want to lose twenty pounds of fat in one month, and I learn that it's not healthy to do so… I'm already setting an expectation for something I don't have the capacity to do while honoring my health. Likewise, in business. If I tell myself I'm going to make $100,000 next month and I've never been able to make $5,000, again, I'm lying to myself about my current capacity and capabilities. Loyalty requires a constant self-check that asks, "Am I able to do this for myself without self-harm? Five months ago

I promised myself these actions, am I still able to carry out these promises? What's changed in my life since the last time I set my goals? Where do I see myself going? What promises have I made to others and am I honoring them?"

Taking these questions into consideration, along with others, will enable you to remain loyal to yourself, and your clients! But this relationship always begins with you. Before someone offers you anything, you should have an idea of how much your work is worth. You should be investing so much into yourself (via practice, coaches, etc) that you can easily say "I'm charging (insert dollar amount) and I know I can execute at that level." Emphasis on knowing you can deliver exactly what you're charging for! I say this because the moment someone desires to work with you and their budget cannot meet your base pay, you must consider what you must let go of in your packaging if you decide to take the client on.. So, if your packaging comes with twelve features and they can only afford seven, you must be sure they're aware of these cuts and changes prior to signing contracts or making verbal agreements. Loyalty in this scenario is clearly communicating all promises, and analyzing whether or not this agreement would better your skillset or potentially hurt your reputation. It's giving them the best of your services at the rate they're able to afford without hurting your pockets, mental stability, and brand name.

But on the reverse, good money doesn't make a mutually beneficial contract either. Let's say an individual approaches you ready to pay the most you've ever made on a single event. Their pockets are full, their hands are ready to sign, and they've even got the deposit ready to be sent. You're giddy and excited about the potential opportunity until you reflect on the connection between you two. After asking yourself some hard questions you realize that they're disrespectful, rigid in thinking, hard to get in contact with, not set on any real ideas, and if they didn't have the money you would have turned them away immediately. Despite the funds, you'd easily be placing yourself in a parasitic situation that could taint your love for creating on behalf of others. Long-term, this decision could be just as dangerous as taking on a client that demands more than what they can afford.

Please, don't abuse your discernment. We've all had situations that we knew wouldn't work out for our bests, yet we ignored ourselves and tried anyway. Doing right by yourself will make you a better service professional for your customers. I know this because in my first two years of business I consistently compromised myself in order to please my clients. And running a business is already costly, but not nearly as much as the years when I hadn't set boundaries and honest expectations of myself and others. I didn't realize what the scripture meant when it said love your neighbor as yourself, not more than yourself. It is true when you hear people say how they became better to work with and their creations excelled when they learned how to charge accordingly and protect themselves in the process. Happier people tend to be better at serving because their cups are far more full than those that burn themselves out. So before you even think about building a brand or re-launching, I need you to take time to ask whether or not you're truly being loyal to yourself and others.Or, are you being loyal for the sake of yourself or other people?

Your Brand Is Just You Personified

Repeat after me, "I am the brand. The brand is me." Now, for the sake of convincing yourself, say it again with 100% more attitude and boldness because it's true! Think about it. Who are your favorite online personalities, business owners, and influencers? I can bet without a shadow of a doubt that you gravitate towards them because you perceive them as showing up as themselves while showcasing how good they are at what they do. It's funny thinking about how we find ourselves overthinking our brands when authenticity is what's drawing us to others'! It's not just the colors, the fonts, and the sales pages. It's who they're showing up as day in and out when they communicate with us. The brand elements are what initially attract us to them, but their personalities and expertise are what keeps us!

But before we go into more detail on what it means to be your brand, let's go ahead and cover the essential branding elements briefly mentioned above.

Every company, no matter the size or influence, has a brand. Every person has the same. To be short, a brand is what you want your audience to know you for. It includes signature fonts, color palettes, logo(s), language tone, potential catchphrases, aka taglines, and mediums used for expression (video, text, still-photos, print, etc). Examples include the Nike swoosh, Eric Thomas's quote, "If you want to succeed as bad as you want to breathe, then you'll be successful" Tiphani Montgomery's use of neon, Courtney Adeleye's hair, and anything else you distinctly remember about a business or personality. The goal of selecting each brand element is to be memorable to your ideal customer while also showcasing who you are. These elements don't have to be extremely specific to the nature of the company, which is why we buy electronics from a company called Apple. But they do need to tell a story that only you're able to tell.

This brings us to the next element of your brand, its unique story. The most successful entrepreneurs have brands that consistently tell the same story over and over again across different messages. Using Nike again, it's the story of perseverance, victory, and consistency. Apple's is luxury, ease, and simplicity. Amazon's is access. Your brand story is what determines what kind of content is relevant for your people. You can consider it a compass if you'd like. It points you in the direction you should go in regard to the who, what, when, where, and how questions that come along with building your brand. That way you're not having to struggle so much with what to say, how to say it, or where to post it. Even still, curating a brand that tells a singular story that resonates is work! No matter how personable you are, it takes skill being able to identify what your vision is but how your ideal customer wants to interact with it. So much skill, if you're not willing to take your time while studying your audience demographics, seeing who they gravitate towards, how you can showcase who you are, and testing out your brand ideas, then my advice would be to hire an expert! Listen, I know we aren't in chapter eight just yet, but do not stress yourself out about branding if you have the resources to hire someone that knows what they're doing! They'll be able to help you uncover your voice, curate a website that converts onlookers into clientele, determine branding colors, logos, fonts, and more.

The amount of detail that goes into curating and sustaining a brand (in your work and online) is what makes it so precious and worthy to be protected. You've got to watch over it the same way you watch over your personal reputation! If you don't like the idea of believing you're a mess, cheap, or diluted in nature, then don't allow yourself to create a brand that leads people to believe so! Come out the gate swinging with your business! It doesn't matter if it costs you $50 to invest in your brand or $5,000, you've got to present yourself how you want to be perceived! So if your goal is to attract high-end clientele, then you've got to meet their expected level of professionalism and expertise. This doesn't mean you can skimp out if your goal is to serve those in a lower socioeconomic status. Less expensive work doesn't equate to cheap services. My encouragement is to take your brand as seriously as you take yourself while crafting it.

Brand Checklist

Optimized Website
Optimized Social Media Bio
Biography
Media Kit
Updated Headshot
Professional Signature
Portfolio

Landing Your Clients

Do not fall for the, "If you build it they'll come" myth. You can build the most amazing brand, but if no one knows that you exist, it doesn't matter. Therefore, all this talk about building a brand and attracting your customers is great and all, but it's pretty pointless if you have no idea how to get clients in the first place. They're necessary because without a website, an email, and eventually a portfolio, you'd be trying to land clients based on a hope and a wish. But once you have these established, it's time to start raising your hand! I know being a sales(wo)man is probably the least of your desired hats, but if you want these invoices to start paying your bills and then some, you must become one. To help you get over your potential fear of salesmanship and pitching, I've decided to give you some simple action items throughout this section.

To start, unlearn what it means to pitch. Sidebar, but haven't you noticed the theme of unlearning throughout this book? It wasn't intentional in the beginning but as I began piecing together each pillar, I realized how much we have to unlearn in order to really understand a concept and master it. Back to topic though, pitching. If you're thinking about the person with the gift of gab or even the cheesy salesman during the midnight hour news, let both ideas go. You don't need to be a smooth talker or sound like a robot to convert clients. What you need are three things, knowing your offer like the back of your hand, patience, and being able to assess gaps, aka needs. This trio will take you places you couldn't have imagined in your business! Let's move forward by breaking each down.

#1 - Knowing your offer like the back of your hand.

The reason pitching can be so difficult is that so many people can't articulate what they're offering in layman's terms. They use language that's familiar with other professionals in their fields, but they can't accurately describe their services using words their customers would resonate with. Essentially, they're overcomplicating a simple conversation by trying to sound more professional, leaving potential customers lost in a hole of confusion. So, ask yourself:

What exactly do I offer?

What do I specialize in?

What size budgets am I willing to work with?

What kind of individual or company do I work with?

What's the least amount of time I require for a project?

Why am I qualified to do what I do?

What are the common words people use to describe my work?

How long have I been in my field?

Do I have resources I can pull in while working on a project?

Taking the time to answer these questions will help you clarify your offer for yourself, especially if you practice reciting the responses to each question. Pro-tip: You can even create a script to help you until you're comfortable with going off your memory.

Practicing with an honest friend will also help set you up for comfortable conversations. Continue to repeat this process until you're using words that highlight your strengths in a way that's digestible, palatable, and understandable to your client. And be sure that you don't feel the pressure of code-switching while doing so. This is a new era, and showing up as yourself (whether it's with an accent, high-pitched or low-pitched voice,) is worth it! Overall, learn to be *professionally* you while talking to potential clients so you don't feel burdened down during calls.

#2 - Patience is key.

Time in itself doesn't improve all things. Having the patience to keep trying while time passes does. This virtue gives you the opportunity to become a master without the rush of self and others. It opens up the possibilities of failure with the aspirations of turning them into successes. As you pitch yourself, you have to understand that this skill is going to take practice before you know: how many calls it takes to convert a client, what kind of person is more apt to invest in your services, and what language resonates the most with your people. Once you realize that pitching is far more about understanding your clientele than it is about securing a contract, watch your conversion rates transform. Patience in pitching says, "I believe I have what this person needs, but let me listen and better understand before I push my services onto them." It also says, "I will contact thirty people this week if that's what it takes to learn." Never forget, it's your business. There's no rush to attain a certain amount of income just because. Take your time, learn your craft, perfect your pitch, and stick with it.

#3 - Become a needs assessor.

Going right in hand with being patient, while you're having contact with potential clients, you're becoming a needs assessor. Why did they contact you? While describing their project, what gaps can you foresee? Do you have the capacity to handle their needs? Is their expectation of this project accurate with their description? Can you efficiently handle this project in their desired timeline? Is there any way you can negotiate the timeline? Being able to ask the right questions while in conversation shows your level of care and your ability to problem-solve. Graciously highlighting the gaps in their idea and showcasing simple solutions builds trust and ultimately makes your conversation stand out from the rest. It also keeps you honest with your capabilities, so you don't corner yourself into believing you must do something for the sake of a check.

Overall, pitching is about relationship building! It's beyond transactional. Find people who have needs you know you can satisfy with your services, and approach them with patience and gratitude as your leads. Even if they don't need you in their current season, go back to our lesson on following-up, and continue to do so, (periodically of course) unless they give you an absolute hell no.

Pitching Checklist

Create a list of ideal customers.
Write down each of their needs and desires.
Reach out to them with your professional email.
Include resources that could help them for free in your initial contact.
Highlight the gap you know you could help address.
Attach your portfolio or at least photos of previous work.
Offer them the chance to speak with you on the phone with specific days and times as options.
Leave your contact information.
Begin your follow-up routine.

CHAPTER 7

Money Matters

At the start, middle, and end of your day; you're running a business now. It doesn't matter if you've generated $10.00 or a hundred thousand, your mindset has to shift from hobbyist to business owner. So say this with me, "If it doesn't make dollars, it doesn't make sense." Giving credit to DJ Quick for this well-known quote, I still find it applicable for CEOs all over. And to be frank, it's a mantra I wish I would've held on to during my early years to say the least. Like many women who start businesses, free or underpriced work was my middle name. I was so giddy about the opportunity to create and serve that I was digging myself into financial holes that took major restructuring to overcome. I was so honored to take on new projects, hitting my revenue goals was a second-thought. It would only sting once I got into the laborious work of being an event planner and realizing my financial input wasn't matching my time output. It wasn't aligning with what I knew I was worth or the creations that I was pouring myself into. So of course, I made some changes that I'd like to share with you. Now, I'm no CPA or financial planner, so I'm only sharing shifts

I've made over the last few years that have helped me take my business from struggling to flourishing.

Understanding Your Money Mindset

Everyone has a relationship with money whether they're conscious of it or not. This relationship presents itself whenever one thinks about money and the feelings they get at the thought. how a person processes outgoing funds and debts, how much they believe they're worthy to make in a year and in one sitting, how they view the rich and the poor, how charitable they're willing to be, and even how much they're willing to charge for their services. Each of these perspectives fuels and motivates us to make financial decisions that we do. If you experience feelings of low-esteem when thinking about finances, then you're more likely to refrain from making long-term investment deals. If you believe debt can be used as a tool, then you're willing to ask the bank for a housing loan to get your first rental property. No matter what decision you're making, it's continuously linked back to your beliefs – aka your mindset. To help reveal your current thoughts, I want you to take the time to reflect on these statements. I also strongly recommend writing or recording your initial thoughts.

> I believe that money is mainly earned through hard work and toil.
>
> Money isn't a priority of mine.
>
> If I had more money, I'd be in a happier situation.
>
> The rich seem to be less humble than the poor.

People should know how to pick themselves up out of financial turmoil by now.

It's okay to do work for free even if it'll cost you in the long run.

My life is a reflection of my financial decisions.

My parents/guardians talked to me about money growing up.

I understood the credit system by the time I was eighteen.

I believe that I'm in a good space financially.

I put a ton of pressure on my business to take care of my bills.

I don't believe in the notion that there's enough money for everyone.

I trust that money is a part of my life covenant.

Being charitable is mandatory.

Discussing money with loved ones is triggering.

I check my bank account on a regular basis with little anxiety.

I trust that my skill set can cover my desired lifestyle.

I'm allowed to amass large sums of money quickly.

I struggle with believing I'm worth charging a high-ticket price tag.

It's not considered a service if you charge a large amount of money for the project.

Take your time while pondering on the sentiments above. Allow each, no matter how triggering, to sit with you for some time. Even go back and see if you gave any contradictory answers during your initial responses. And based on what you see about yourself, how would you rate your current money mindset?

0 = Broken; high-anxiety, limiting beliefs, low sense of self-worth, money is hard, no money to be charitable with, and ability to generate income.

1 = Poor; limiting beliefs, willing to be charitable, views the rich or poor in a negative light, not willing to take any calculated bets on self, hard to obtain and keep money.

2 = Moderate; money can be a tool but it's hard to acquire, charitable, some money anxiety, skills might be able to generate money but isn't sure.

3 = Good; money is a tool, worthy of making money but not comfortable with high-ticketed rates, debt can be a resource or avoided, low money-anxiety, willing to take calculated financial risks, not as strategic as I could be with revenue goals.

4 = Healthy; loves giving, holds no negative stereotype against the rich nor poor, able to charge based on value, healthy relationship with debt, openly discusses money, able to check any financial anxiety, trusts in skill set, believes in self, obtaining money with ease is a right.

To add an extra layer of self-awareness, you can ask the closest person to you whether or not the score you gave yourself matches what they've seen through your habits. Remember, the goal is to get clear on how you feel about money, including your relationship with it. Without this, your journey to financial freedom through your business and future investments will be prolonged.

Refreshing Your Money Mindset

"A feast is made for laughter,

wine makes life merry,

and money is the answer for everything.

Do not revile the king even in your thoughts,

or curse the rich in your bedroom,

because a bird in the sky may carry your words,

and a bird on the wing may report what you say."

Ecclesiastes 10:19-20

Money is a crucial asset to life. As we see in Ecclesiastes chapter ten, it's considered a tool used to answer the issues that present themselves in this lifetime. It is not a savior, but it is leverage. For a moment, I want you to reflect on all of your life's dreams. Relish in them and when you finish, continue reading on.

Now that you've had a moment to visualize, I'd like to ask you this question. How many of your life's dreams require absolutely zero dollars to accomplish? Likely, the answer is none. Even falling in love with your future spouse comes with a price tag like gas, internet service, or whatever necessary resources you'll need to meet them. So, if you believe you'll be able to get by in this life in the kinds of nations we live in, without any source of income, well, reality is soon to set in. Because Ecclesiastes made it clear that money is the answer to all things, but it did not tell us to fall in love with it. You don't fall in love with a house because it provides shelter, in the same way, you don't fall in love with any other tool you're blessed with. On the contrary, you respect them and give them each a proper place in your world. Your finances are no different. Thus, aspiring to amass great wealth makes you no less humble, nor does it put you in line to be a sinner. No, aspiring to amass great wealth reveals your inner desires and hopefully at your core, to be a servant to those in need and to set a legacy for those that'll come after you (whether you birthed them, raised them, or mentored them).

This is where your refresher course begins. The first thing we're going to tackle is your need to do things for free or cheap. How in the world are you going to hit your revenue goals if you continue to undersell yourself? Listen to me when I say there is no room for "free" or "cheap" when the opportunity won't provide you with longstanding benefits. It's a hard reality to take in, but you won't start making more money until you start requiring it for yourself! Setting lofty goals like hitting six-figures for the first time in your family line won't cut it. You have to go out and know that you're worth six-figures and more. Then, you have to charge prices that'll get you there.

Trust me when I say I understand how much rejection comes with making shifts like this. But if you're going to play small for the rest of your life, why force yourself to carry such weighty dreams? Is it not better for your health to ensure your efforts match your desires? So what if you get 100 no's in a month while pitching your services and new pricing? On ask number 101, you could hit your sales goal for the month if the project's big enough! Wealth generation is a game of numbers beloved. You try, and you try until you finally start getting it right, and you repeat! You'll begin to learn what's keeping you from landing deals. You'll even see how many no's it takes before you land a yes on average (your conversion rate for success). Even your self-respect will increase because you'll know you're out here earning every single dollar that you're bringing in.

Now, for those who equate impact with a price tag, let this be a reminder. People never feel cheated on paying your invoice when you deliver excellent and memorable work. It might have made them feel like they were challenging themselves by agreeing, but in the end, they're most worried about working with the business that'll best execute their ideas. So no, free and cheap don't mean you'll have a greater emotional impact on the client. In certain cases, it can guarantee that you'll be the one suffering the most in the deal.

Setting Your Numbers

If you're wondering how you can set your revenue goals, I want you to use the following questions to guide you:

1: How much are your monthly expenses? What's the least amount of money you spend in order to live? This includes rent, mortgage, loans, debts, food, gas, etc.

2: What's the most amount of money you've ever made in a year from your skillset (not paid by a job)?

3: What's the most amount of money you've ever made in a single month from your skillset?

4: How much money do you currently make (can include your job here)?

5: How much money does it take you to run your business from month to month? Include business apps, certifications, etc.

6: How much are you currently charging for your services?

7: How much are your competitors charging?

8: How many projects do you have the capacity to take on per month?

9: How much will you have to pay in taxes a year based on your current income?

Your answer to number one sets your bare minimum revenue goal for the year, and I do mean bare minimum! This shouldn't be your target goal. Looking at your responses to numbers two through nine, you'll be able to see what you currently have the capacity to strive for on top of this minimum goal. For example, if your lifestyle costs you $3,000 per month, then $36,000 per year is your base. If you've been able to make more than this on your own, then your minimum shifts to that number, let's say it's $42,000. If you've never made a steady income via entrepreneurship, you'll stick with your lifestyle minimum. Next, you'll look at how many projects you can complete in a month's time that gives you the space to still breathe and take care of yourself. From here, you'll total how much it takes you to run your business every month. The reason I want you to use these numbers to create a revenue goal is so you're giving your revenue an actual job. Wanting to make a hundred thousand dollars isn't impossible, but it's a hell of a lot harder to do when you've never learned how to make enough to continue sustaining yourself first. This business is yours, so there's no rush to become wealthy. I'm not saying it'll take years to do, but I am saying you have to see this as a way to improve your skills. If you can handle your smaller financial goals, how much more efficient will you be when it comes to scaling and making two-fold? Referring back to your numbers: if your lifestyle minimum is $36,000 and let's say it doesn't cost you anything to run your business (yet), to challenge yourself, I'd say add $15,000 on top. This money will be used for emergencies, business expenses, investments, and of course, saving to file your taxes!

At $51,000 in this example of a yearly sales goal, you're pushing to bring in approximately $12,750 per quarter or $4,250 per month. To be clear, having lower revenue goals such as this does not mean you can revert back to charging pennies. It means you charge premium prices because you don't have the capacity to take on more projects. And depending on your tenacity with learning, pitching, and putting yourself in the right opportunities, you could fulfill this before the year even ends! And I mean this no matter if you're aiming for $51,000 or $510,000! Being clear about how much money you want to make, giving it defined terms and jobs, and charging according to how much capacity you have, breeds a financial environment that welcomes in abundance.

***

Switching our focus to invoice systems, I'll spend some time discussing when to send an invoice instead of advising you on which system to use. Depending on where you are in the world, you'll need to make this decision for yourself. So whether you choose

Quickbooks or stick with Business PayPal, the advice to follow will apply the same.

I'm a firm believer in deposits. This is because they show a level of commitment from your client that separates them from those that are simply wasting your time. It also makes sure that you're not waiting until the end of a project to receive complete payment. No matter how sweet your clients may seem, some people will try and scam you out of deserved payments. To protect yourself, I say take between a 20 to a 50 percent deposit upfront before the start of any services. Include this in your contracts and verify on the phone and via email that they understand this requirement. As for completed projects, you'll ultimately make the decision on when you want to be paid the remaining balance. Some people wait until the day of the event, some even require payment 1 to 4 weeks before the project due date (depending on the length of the project). My recommendation is to make this decision based on the average length of your projects in comparison to your monthly sales goals. If you're able to wait until the project completion, you can do so. If it's more beneficial to get the final payment before the event date, then choose this as your option.

***

For the last segment of this section on money matters, I'm going to outline what you need to do to protect yourself in the long run. There's a messy habit new business owners adapt that makes them believe that because they're earning their money legally, they can store it how they want and don't have to worry about their trails. Let me tell you right now that is a lie. Making money, especially in countries like the United States, requires precaution and systems that prove your legality. To help you, and keep it simple, I've devised a checklist below of systems you need to have in order to show that you're legit.

Insert X if applicable	
	Open an LLC or C-Corp
	File for an EIN number
	Open a business checking account
	Open a business invoicing system (Example: Quickbooks)
	Open a taxes savings account
	Set yourself up as an employee of your business
	Start paying yourself via a salary from your business account

CHAPTER 8

Art of Delegation

I meet so many people, especially Black women, that believe they have to do everything on their own if they want something to get done correctly. We can analyze where this belief stems from another day (especially the racial implications behind it). But for now, let me remind you that this belief system is the biggest lie of all, especially in business. Not done by you does not translate to not done correctly. And because we're a group of people that believe in accountability, we understand that the failure to trust in others to do their work is a direct reflection of ourselves and our communication skills. As your virtual mentor, I'll be the first to admit that I'm not the queen of delegation – yet. But I do know that it's something that will help determine whether your life and your business sink or swim.

You've made it to the last chapter of this book, so I'm sure you've caught on to how much I like to have you repeat statements. Today's reading is no different. I want you to say this out loud:

Asking for help doesn't make me lazy.

Asking for help proves I'm a genius and a hard worker.

Although I'm not necessarily someone that believes there's no such thing as laziness I don't believe needing help falls into that category (or is anywhere near it, to be frank). I believe needing someone else's skills and talents is a tool God gave us to keep us in community. Imagine if an individualistic society actually thrived. If no one needed anyone, who would we depend on? How would we remain humble? What would be the point of uniquely made people if we could do it all alone? To me, that sounds like a world that's gone gray. A community that's lost its luster and based on how we currently live, would likely turn into a life of competition and greed. This is why even in countries like the United States, where we claim to be individualistic, we still understand that collectivism is the way to any kind of mass success. We don't expect one person to run a multi-billion dollar corporation, yet we think we can wear seventy hats in our own lives and remain sane.

Life doesn't work like that. There's no need to force yourself to wear every hat in your business, maintain a household, be your own trainer, a stable family member, friend, personal chef, etc. And if no one's ever told you that you don't have to do it all to have it all, let me be the first. You have the right to do the least, at your best, so you can yield the most. Let me break that down so you can envision it. Doing the most is a concept that we're letting go of this year. Mentor after mentor has reminded me that working hard isn't what makes anyone profitable. It's being able to get your business rolling and work efficiently. This doesn't imply that the work that comes along with being efficient isn't complicated. Instead, it hints at the importance of learning how to get over your obstacles quicker and with the least amount of toil as possible. So by you doing the least, you're not all of a sudden becoming a lazy and downtrodden worker. On the contrary, less work should translate to more meaningful work. This to-do list should be completed with excellence with the expectation of yielding the most amount of fruit. Quite literally, it goes from forcing yourself to try and accomplish fifteen things in a day to doing the five most important tasks that could change your life.

It might seem that I'm pushing this paradigm shift with a heavy hand, but it's because I'm passionate about remaining alive long enough to witness the changes we've been working for. We know we can't add a single day to our lifespan, but we sure as heck can take away. And it's because of superwoman syndrome, the belief that you must do everything alone, that women (mainly Black women) are experiencing underlying health conditions that are killing us.[3] Too much stress is causing our bodies to shut down on us before we get to see the changes we've been seeking. And I don't know about you, but God willing, I'd like to be able to make it into the promised land and not die off because of my ill-begotten choices.

It's time for us to start looking at the micro-duties in our lives with as much care as the macro-duties. This would require us to see the importance of partnership, collaboration, and teamwork

---

3 https://www.ncbi.nlm.nih.gov/pmc/articles/PMC3072704/

inside of our lives and not just in political matters that impact the country.

What Does It Mean To Delegate?

According to Oxford Dictionary, delegation means to entrust (a task or responsibility) to another person, typically one who is less senior than oneself. In other words, it means to intentionally ask someone for their help. To be even more specific, it involves being clear about what you want, how you want it done and the time-line. What I've found over the years is that delegation in this way becomes an art form dependent upon effective communication between two or more parties. And the one who should be the over-communicator and aware is who's in need of the help, not the service party. Here's what I mean… If I'm in need of a custom meal service, I must first recognize what I absolutely love and hate, why I struggle with making my own meals, any unhealthy eating habits I may have and so forth. I must then communicate this to my service provider so they have a foundation to lean on to under-stand my eating preferences. From here, I need to know how many meals I need them to prepare in a week, based on how many meals I consume in a day. Also, do they need to provide snack options or drinks, and of course, when I'd like them to deliver my meals or what day I prefer to pick them up. Again, it's my responsibility to be the over-communicator here because I'm the one that needs the help. I can't provide bare minimum information and expect them to meet my every need. Over-communicating because you over-stand your needs is how you can differentiate between a bad ser-vice provider and someone who just didn't understand what little you offered them. And no, becoming this person doesn't make you difficult and hard to work with. Quite the opposite! Those who you decide to work with will be extremely grateful that you know what you want, unlike so many people.

So when should you ask for help?

Certainly not after needing it for weeks or even months. Ideally, you create a delegation plan for your life after reviewing your personal strengths and weaknesses. Again, this is for your life not just your business. To make it a little easier on you I've drafted a list of questions you can ask yourself in regard to both categories (life and business).

Day to Day Life Questions

Question	Yes or No
Do I enjoy any housekeeping chores? If so, which ones?	
Are there household duties I prefer not to do? If yes, which ones?	
Do I have enough time in a week to prepare my own meals without stress?	
Do I have anyone in my home that can help me maintain it? If so, are they stressed by the idea of home maintenance?	
Do I have anyone I can take my emotions to and get professional insight on?	
Do I have a system that helps me keep track of what I need to be doing on a day to day basis?	
Do I have any major life responsibilities that continually take time away from me working on my business?	
If I had help in any of the areas above, would I improve on how much time I have for myself?	

Business Life Questions

Question	Yes or No
Do I get to spend most of my time building my business instead of running day to day functions?	
Are there specific tasks I absolutely can't stand doing inside of my business? If yes, which are they?	
Do I enjoy marketing tasks?	
Am I strong at pitching this company? Am I allocating enough time to pitch?	
Can I consistently make graphics that resonate with my audience?	
Do I have enough time in a week to make content for my audiences online?	
Do I have a secure financial system for my business that makes tax season less of a pain?	
Am I consistently clearing out my inbox and getting back to clients and potential prospects?	
Am I dedicated to getting my company the appropriate media attention it needs on a consistent basis?	
Am I good at handling the tech issues that come with running my business?	

Remember that these questions are just to get you started. You've got to go deep here and really uncover your skills, talents, and yes, even preferences. I recognize that this might not be the messaging you're seeing online from other business coaches. We live in a time where the value of mentorship and coaching have skyrocketed, thus influencing people to believe they just need a coach for every area of their lives. This simply isn't true. As a business coach, I know how vital it is to have someone in your corner who can help you avoid potential pitfalls. Still, we don't have to be masters of everything. Don't you remember the quote, "A jack of all trades is a master of none?" Well, this truth didn't disappear when coaches of all kinds began to pop-up. Those who tend to understand this most are wealthy. Spending ample amounts of time trying to unlearn a weakness instead of spending time amplifying your strengths is a misallocation of time management.

The goal is to always get more of our time back so we can spend it living, not just doing. This is a mindset of the privileged. Cash comes and goes, but time ceases to exist almost within the same second it's present. And no matter how much you try and force yourself to be all things, you can't. No one can. This isn't a measure of instability. It's a recognition of reality. I remember hearing a woman who runs a multi-million dollar micro-brand do a Periscope talk where she was covering how she makes at least $80,000 per month. For context, this is a Black woman in her mid-thirties with two children and a remarkable online reputation. Of course, someone asked her what her best hires were that changed the trajectory of her company, and she confidently responded by saying, "Hiring a cleaning service changed my life." She didn't say a Chief

Marketing Officer. She didn't mention a financial planner. She said it was a cleaning service. For everything else relevant to her brand she enjoys contractual hiring because she doesn't want to run a major corporation, she just wants to make the most amount of money while staying in her own zone of genius.

Talk about knowing what and when to delegate. Reflect on the largest consumers of your time and ask whether or not they contribute to you making an impact, living a sustainable lifestyle, and making money. If not, this could be an area you let go of in exchange for peace of mind. These decisions will help you trade-off busy work for productive work. Now, I know there are potential obstacles that can keep you from delegating. I completely understand that it does take an ounce of privilege to be able to do this, but listen to me when I say, it only requires just that; an ounce. Although I'm encouraging you to take tasks off of your plate, I'm not telling you how much to spend while doing it. I'm only emphasizing how worthwhile it's going to be!

Maybe you can't do a meal planning service, but you could use curbside pick-up or delivery. Spending money on a weekly cleaner might hit the bank too hard, but what about a monthly contractor? Hiring a graphic designer might be way outside of your budget for now, but finding a trusted contractor on Fiverr would save you time and money as projects pop up. Even aside from these quick fixes, did you know you can even hire someone to write out your business and marketing plan without having to make them an employee? So the excuse of wanting to start another business but not having the time to properly outline it disappears. Not being able to hire them today doesn't dissolve this solution either. This is where savings goals come into play! Don't continue setting yourself up to be the only one maintaining your business, your health, and your sanity. You've got to make a real effort to transition out of being Superwoman. To be great at what you do, you need the time to be able to do it. So no, you don't need to become an expert home keeper, marketer, financial analyst or coder in order to become one of the greats. You simply need to be who you were destined to be. And I genuinely don't believe any of us were created to be masters of all.

If you don't take anything else away from this chapter, remember that you cannot leave yourself bogged down in the miscellaneous tasks of running a business. Learn to ask for help and do it ahead of time! So when emergencies do pop-up, people are far more willing to work with you because you're not known for running them into the ground. In addition, you have to continually ask for help. This isn't some kind of one-off task. People don't jump at the opportunity to help you when they believe you're doing just fine. Check your entire ego at the door when it comes to this matter. You have to raise your hand and keep raising it. And when you do, make sure you're giving your service providers everything they need to succeed (and replace them quickly if they continually fail). Celebrate them for their work, and celebrate yourself for asking. Use incentives to keep your people motivated and see their expertise as an incentive to your own life. But if you're genuinely finding yourself having the hardest time with delegating and knowing who and when to hire, you can invest in a Delegation Coach. This is someone who trains you to think more efficiently and see where you can let go.

However, just like I mentioned earlier, you don't need a coach for everything. Try this on your own first, but if you don't see any changes in your stress levels after sixty days, invest in a coach that'll help you overcome this mental roadblock.

Conclusion

As I finish this manuscript, I admit that the gift I have has never been about me. I am merely a vessel being used to fulfill my assignment. The creativity that I have is from a long line of very resourceful and creative ancestors. Once I realized that my passion is to breathe life into extraordinary experiences from ordinary resources, I allowed myself to flow. You see, this book is about serving those who dare to be different. Yes, I'm talking about you! That's right, you see life every day as an event, and you don't miss the opportunity to give that wonderful experience to others. The world needs and yearns for it, and who are we to deprive them. I want to thank all those that have taken the journey to read, learn from my lessons, and go out and create those W O W experiences.

Acknowledgments

I am thankful to GOD for entrusting me with my gifts and talents. To my grandmother, Sarah Jenkins, for shaping and molding me (I know you're looking on from high with a smile), my parents Robert L Jenkins Sr. and Evelyn Jenkins for never giving up on me and being my number one fans in my club of three. My baby boy who will always be my baby, Robert, your encouragement is beyond measure. Finally, my long-lasting forever-friend and business partner Kairi A. Hunter, CHBH Events Creative Director, thank you for seeing the vision and adding your extra spark to every event.

Author Mini-Bio

Valerie Jenkins is the CEO of Creative Hands By Him (CHBH) Events, which is a successful full-service event planning company founded in New York City with an international reach. Her entrepreneurial spirit, combined with years of experience, serves as a great source of inspiration for forward-thinkers looking to bring their own event planning companies to fruition.

About The Book

The Three B's is a book of wisdom for those looking to build their business, bank account, and legacy via event planning. In these pages you'll find stories and strategies directly from the life of Valerie Jenkins, CEO of Creative Hands By Him Events, a successful full-service event planning company. As her debut book, The Three B's serves as an additional resource Ms. Jenkins offers her audience in hopes of inspiring them to go after who they truly are, and what they know they deserve. Unlike other business books for event planners, this one uses storytelling in order to put you in the shoes of Valerie as she walked along her early years. Because real stories allow us to see the *how* in business instead of only knowing *what*. The Three B's is concise and full of advice that you can immediately begin implementing in your own business and life.